Donated by

Minibook Publ. Co.

Montgomery, WV.

© DEMCO, INC. 1990 PRINTED IN U.S.A.

Self-Excellence

*Key To
Preventive Stress Management
& Goal-Oriented Living*

Self-Excellence

Key To Preventive Stress Management & Goal-Oriented Living

S. A. Swami, Ph.D.
Professor of Civil Engineering
West Virginia Institute of Technology

Minibook Publishing Co.
Montgomery, WV

All rights reserved. No part of this book may be reproduced or transmitted in any form or by any means, electronic or mechanical, including photocopying, recording or by any information storage or retrieval system without written permission from the author, except for the inclusion of brief quotations in a review.

Library of Congress Cataloging-in-Publication Data

Swami, S.A. (Shanmugam A.), 1928-
  Self-excellence: key to preventive stress management & goal-oriented living.

  Bibliography: p.
  Includes Index.
  1. Stress (Psychology)—Prevention. 2. Self-realization. 3. Goal (Psychology) I. Title.
BF575.S75S93   1987   158'.1   87-5578

ISBN 0-941553-00-0

Printed in the United States of America

Respectfully dedicated to my teachers:

Prof. William H. Goetz
and
Prof. C. G. Swaminathan

Acknowledgment

I owe it to my employer, West Virginia Institute of Technology, for providing me the opportunity to develop the concept of *self-excellence* through the Department of Continuing Education.

I am sincerely grateful to Ms. Debra Cook, Assistant Professor of English, West Virginia Institute of Technology, for her untiring and enthusiastic support in the preparation of the manuscript and in copyediting the text. Special thanks go to Dr. Virginia Gray, Professor of English, West Virginia Institute of Technology, for her constructive criticisms in the preparation of the manuscript. I am also thankful to Ms. Julia Brown for her assistance in copyediting.

I am particularly thankful to Ms. Margaret Queen, ballet teacher, for her elegant pictures depicting the various exercise and Yoga postures and to Ms. Cathy Lynch, art teacher, for her beautiful illustrations.

Special thanks are due to Dr. Rafiqul Molla, Professor of Printing Technology, West Virginia Institute of Technology, for his valuable advice and assistance throughout the project. All the photographs in this book were shot by him in his studio.

I am thankful to my wife, Anusuya, and our son, Jay, for their patience and assistance in the various phases of this project.

What is new in this book?

Cognitive distortion

50% Elevated cardiopulmonary balance (50% ECP balance)

Emotional turbidity

Self-excellence

7 Laws of human behavior

7 Laws of stress

7 Laws of success

Uniqueness characteristic of the mind

Contents

Preface:
How This Book Was Written and Why

PART 1—Self-Excellence Versus Stress

1 The Road Ahead: The Search for Self-Excellence in a World of Stress 3
- The stress of life
- The meaning of stress
- The road ahead—Life is to live
- Secondary evolution
- Concept of self and stress
- Homeostasis and equanimity
- The meaning of self-excellence

2 The Triumph of Self-Excellence over Stress 9
- Man the microcosm and the universe the macrocosm
- The human body as a path
- The human mind
- Uniqueness characteristic of the mind
- Role of individual effort
- The power of self-excellence
- Validity of self-excellence in the modern world

PART 2—All About Stress

3 The Stress of Life   **19**
- Definition of stress
- Subjective nature of stress
- 7 Universal laws of stress
- Signs of stress in a person
- Stress in daily life
- Stress and your emotions

4 Physiological Aspects of Stress   **25**
- Emotions and endocrine glands
- Hypothalamus: the supreme body-mind bridge
- The stress hormones
- Stress and the nervous system
- Stress and brain waves
- Stress and the fight-or-flight response
- Stress and artery spasm

5 Psychological Aspects of Stress   **39**
- Stress and your mind
- The Omega effect
- Conflict in the mind
- Mechanism of stress response
- Frustration and stress
- Anxiety and stress

6 Stress-Related Ailments   **47**
- Body-mind partnership
- High blood pressure, *the silent killer*
- Stress and your heart
- Stress and stroke

- Stress and kidney failure
- Stress and peptic ulcer
- Stress and headache

7 Classification and Sources of Stress   **61**
- Short-term physical stress
- Long-term physical stress
- Anger provoking stress
- Fear provoking stress
- Grief provoking stress
- Joy provoking stress
- Anxiety provoking stress
- Personality

PART 3—All About Self-Excellence

8 Stumbling Blocks Preventing Self-Excellence   **73**
- Lack of purpose in life
- Lack of will and discipline
- Laziness and procrastination
- Lack of self-respect
- Lack of patience
- Emotional turbidity
- Cognitive distortion

9 Mainsprings of Self-Excellence   **81**
- Self-confidence
- Planned continuous learning
- Commitment and willingness to work
- Motivation and enthusiasm
- Willingness to forego immediate pleasures
- Emotion management
- Reaching out to help others

PART 4—5 Steps to Self-Excellence

10 **Step 1—Towards Bodily Excellence**   **91**
    Through the Pulsative 20 Minutes
- 50% Elevated cardiopulmonary balance
- Isometric exercises
- Isotonic exercises
- Aerobic exercises
- Rope jumping—the perfect exercise
- Hatha Yoga
- Relaxation sports

11 **Step 2—Towards Mental Excellence and Positive**   **113**
    Self-Image Through the Meditative 20 Minutes
- Meaning of meditation
- Meditation and brainwaves
- Self-acceptance through auto-suggestion
- Contemplation
- Self-psychoanalysis
- Visualization
- Desensitization
- The Relaxation Response

12 **Step 3—Towards Goals-Achieving Excellence**   **131**
    Through the Creative 20 Minutes
- Principles of goal setting
- Stumbling blocks to success
- 7 Laws of success
- Visualization
- Skill-learning
- Overlearning
- Role-playing

13 Step 4—Towards Excellence in Interpersonal Relations   141
- 7 Laws of human behavior
- 7 Principles of interpersonal relations
- Assertiveness
- How to deal with difficult people
- How to hold the friendship
- How to heal strained relations
- Accept what you can not change

14 Step 5—Towards Excellence in Eating and Drinking Habits   153
- Effect of stress on eating
- 2 Deadly enemies: cholesterol and triglyceride
- Low salt diet
- Balanced diet
- Stress, alcohol, and relaxation
- Dangers of alcohol
- Intelligent drinking

15 Drugs and Smoking—Their Effects on the Body   167
- Stress, drugs, and relaxation
- Dangers of drug addiction
- Stress, smoking, and relaxation
- Smoking and heart problems
- The Surgeon General's warning

Epilog   173
References   177
Glossary   181
Index   191
About the Author   197
Colophon

PREFACE

How This Book Was Written—and Why

The day was September 7, 1964, and I had just then landed in New York airport after a weary journey from India. One more time my trembling fingers felt my pocket for the money I had with me, $8.00! That was all the money I had for the beginning of a new life in the land of free will and opportunities. Well, that was not all; I had faith in me, and faith in the people around me, and I had a burning desire to learn—to learn about everything that I needed to know for professional and personal advancement. I also had visions for a happy and healthy living for the future.

Thus, I started my life in the United States of America as a graduate student at Purdue. Different educational systems, cultural conflicts, financial constrictions, and pressure to achieve all began to have their share of stress on me. There were many sleepless nights. I began to wonder how to cope with my problems. I could not help thinking whether it was wise on my part to throw away a high paying job and a life of security in India for the sake of professional growth in a far-off land. **Dale Carnegie's** strategy came to my mind: What worse can now happen? It has already happened; pick up the pieces and plan for the future. How wise his words sounded to me—particularly when I had no money for the return fare to India!

What kind of plan do I need? Of course, it should be one that suits my aims, ambitions, aspirations and their fulfillment, leading to a life of vibrant health and true happiness so that I get the most out of living. It should be a coordinated plan for living where I could blossom to my full potential.

Where do I find such a plan? I began to spend countless hours in the library sifting through each and every self-help book that I can lay my hands on, which promised to change the life of the reader, and began to study books on philosophy, psychology and religion which promised to enrich the reader's life. While these books were either informative, academic, or scholarly, none of them satisfied my need. Nevertheless, they helped me to carry on my burdens of the day with a grin on my face.

After the successful completion of the graduate program, I settled down to a career of teaching civil engineering in the West Virginia Institute of Technology, and I began again my quest for a philosophy of living better suited to the modern times. I widened my field of search to the fields of biology, physiology, sociology and cosmology. It was a relentless but fascinating search. I began to examine my own life and behavior, and those of the people around me. At times it was bewildering to look at the problems of the society—divorce, alcohol and drugs, teen-age promiscuity, unemployment, financial troubles, physical and mental sicknesses, obsessions for success and money, and other violent crimes on the city streets. At times it was confusing. Why are there so many problems in a land of plenty, opulence, and opportunities?

Hans Selye's *"Stress of Life"* began to make more sense to me than ever before, as it gently unfolded the meaning of the general adaptation syndrome and the psychosomatic role stress played on the individual. If there is stress, there must be ways and means of managing, or even preventing it before it gets the better of me. So I began to scan the books in the library on stress and its management. I started reading everything that was related to stress. Literally every popular magazine from *Times* to *Reader's Digest* carried articles on stress. Every now and then articles on stress appeared in the local newspapers. Advertisements for stress seminars and workshops were found all over the country. Conducting "in-house" stress workshops became the style of the day with large corporations and offices of employment primarily for the white-collar employees and executives. With a view to learn the "secrets" of stress management, I enrolled in one of the seminars conducted in a top-class hotel for a reasonable fee.

As a result of all this experience, I presume that I have gathered more information on stress management than most experts. However, when I tried to relate the many techniques of stress management to my personal way of life, I found that they were primarily aimed at the symptoms of stress, and not the cause. There was a missing link.

Stress, being a subjective phenomenon, needs a subjective inquiry for effective management. It dawned on me that the missing link is the

PREFACE

excellence of the subjective self, or *"self-excellence"* in one word. Keeping the self-excellence in the core, I began to synthesize and formulate an action plan for my own creative living and preventive stress management—a plan that I was after. From this synthesis emerged a picture of the total spectrum of life in all its splendour and glory, as far as I can see from birth to death—myself as an individual, my role in the social milieu, and my place in the cosmic wholeness. It was like the emergence of the true picture of a 1000-pieces puzzle when all the pieces fall in place. In the center of this picture was "I", and everything in my life was built around this "I". No book on stress management presented such a holistic perspective of the individual's life. When viewed through the cosmic identity the human life lasts but a fleeting moment in the vastness of the cosmic eternity. But yet, this "moment" of living is long enough to be of significance to the "I".

Behind this "I" lies the conscious and subconscious mind of the person. **Sigmund Freud** called it the "iceberg" to emphasize the mostly hidden and unknown aspects of the mind. All the potentials and elements for a happy and healthy living are lying dormant in the mind waiting to be unearthed—by self-effort! I have to do it myself, and no body else can do it for me! The effort is to be aimed at excellence—excellence of the subjective self and, thereby, excellence in the objective world.

I began to read through scores of biographies of successful people in every field to learn how they achieved excellence in their lives. I was looking for that something which they had applied to their living and which others had not. Soon I discovered that the "secrets" of their success lay in their endeavors to excel themselves in their chosen fields of interest. Does it sound simple?

No man is an island. There is a constant need for interaction with other people in the family, office, and the outside world. The more I observed, the more clearly I found that one of the major causes of stress for most people is their inability to relate to other people. Excellence in living is impaired by a poor interpersonal relationship. Once again I began to search books on psychology and human behavior for clues of excellence in interpersonal relationship.

Thus, finally emerged an integrated plan for living—for me, with self-excellence at the core. I began to practice this plan as a way of life. It did not take long to see the effects. I was beginning to feel at ease at situations which used to be stressors for me before. The goals I had set and worked for were achieved slowly and steadily, which, in turn, led to further goals in personal and professional life. My health improved. I was able to relax, bodily and mentally, and began to sleep well. My blood pressure fell to the normal range of values for my age. I found time to stop and stare at the birds and flowers, and at the sky and the stars. Above all, I began to enjoy my work in the office. In fact, I began to look forward to the dawn of the morrow which became an additional day of adventure in living.

I was so pleased with the results and with myself that I decided to share it with like-minded people in the community who might be looking for betterment in their living. At my initiative the first clinic on self-excellence and stress management was offered to the general public in 1974 through the Office of Continuing Education of the West Virginia Institute of Technology. It was an instant success. The interest it generated became the motive force for successive clinics, seminars and workshops every year since then. It is the feedback from these courses over the years that finally convinced me that the subject matter of the course should be shared with a larger section of the community in the form of a book.

A former student, a woman in her forties, one day greeted me on the street, and told me that she was at cross roads in her life when she attended the very first seminar. By virtue of her listening in the class, she was able to make the proper decision for better future living. She then profusely thanked me and disappeared in the crowd. Another woman got back to her first love, piano, which she had left since high school, and has now become a proficient player "enjoying every minute of her life", as she put it, "after rediscovering her creative potential." An officer in the coal mines who attended the class went on to organize effective interpersonal working groups by virtue of his change in attitudes and increased sensitivity to other human beings. These are but a few of the true feedbacks, which gave me the encouragement to take up the book-writing project.

Since the course was offered continuously for more than a decade, it gave me ample opportunity to revise, enlarge and accommodate the latest research findings in the areas of health, behavior and nutrition, which form an integral part of our living. The book is thus a product of evolution over two decades of research and development, and, above all, it is based on personal experience.

I have tried to emphasize and explain the cause and effect of events wherever possible. It is my firm belief that changes in our attitudes and voluntary adaptations in our behavior are easier only when we realize the cause and effect of the stressors, ourselves, rather than being told, and that our very thought process, itself, is strongly conditioned by such self-realizations.

I want to assure you that if you are determined to make the most of your life, managing your stresses effectively, developing your hidden potentials, and fulfilling life's aims, ambitions and aspirations, this book holds the key.

You did not take this book to read about how it was written. Please go ahead with your reading and help yourself to excellence in living. After reading the first two chapters, if you are not inspired to know more about the 5-steps to self-excellence as a way of life, then toss this book into the trash can. You don't need it.

Montgomery, WV S. A. Swami
April 15, 1987

PART 1

Self-Excellence Versus Stress

Chapter 1

The Road Ahead: The Search for Self-Excellence In a World of Stress

"All I can say is that the philosophy of stress has helped me enormously in achieving equanimity and a personally satisfactory program for the way I want to go through life. I rather think if you tried it, it might help you too."

Hans Selye
Author of *The Stress of Life*

"The road ahead," so concluded **Dr. Hans Selye** in his remarkable book, *The Stress of Life,* after revealing how the study of stress deals with the defense mechanisms of our own body. As he saw it, man's ultimate aim is *to express himself as fully as possible, according to his own lights.* The goal is not certainly to avoid stress. Stress is part of life. "But, in order to express yourself fully, you must find out your optimum stress-level, and then, use your adaptation energy at a rate and in a direction adjusted to the innate structure of your mind and body."

It is here our book begins. You can not live my life, and I can not live yours. We are all different. The only thing we have in common is our need to obey certain biological laws which govern all human beings and the dormant desire for self-expression deep within us constantly seeking opportunities for manifestation during the process of our living.

The Stress of Life

I am sure that you have contemplated your own life. There were times when you wished how different things were whenever you were driven to the extremes of your emotions like anger, fear, or grief. There were also times when you wished how nice would it have been if those people such as your spouse, a teenaged son or daughter, or some one in the office did things always your way. How much you wished you had some more money so that you could buy that dream car of yours or the colonial type house you want to live in. How much you wished you could afford the Hawaiian vacation this coming summer, so the list of wishes can go on and on.

You have had worries and frustrations. There were times when you could not sleep thinking about the events at the office, anticipating the threatened lay-off, meeting dead-lines, and having to work in a new section under a boss whom you hated. There were times when you came home with a splitting head-ache and aching body muscles. There were times when you were tense and "keyed-up," yelling at your spouse and children, not knowing what happened to you.

You have experienced a variety of emotions. How mad you were at your spouse the other day for whatever reason. How angry you were at your supervisor or boss in the office the other day and felt like hitting him but could not. How mad you were at your neighbor when you found that he had encroached a few feet onto your land with his newly erected fence. How grief-stricken you were that day when your beloved got killed in the automobile accident. How helpless and miserable you felt when you found that the one person whom you loved most had become an alcoholic.

Well, my reader, please bear with me. It is not my intention to paint a gloomy picture of the mundane life, but it is only with a view to throw the spotlight on the common undercurrent in the living process of human beings which, by now, you would have recognized as the stress of life. Ours, no doubt, is a world of stress!

The Meaning of Stress

Stress, to start with, is a subjective phenomenon. It is the adaptation response of living organisms to changing environments that threaten their survival. In humans this response is processed through the nervous system, and the outcome, as far as that individual is concerned, is labelled as "stress." The circumstances that initiate this response are termed as "stressors."

Stress is a non-specific response in the sense that it can not be pin-pointed as a universal cause-and-effect phenomenon. It may vary from person to person. What is stressful to one, may not be stressful to another, but may even be invigorating to yet another. Stress, therefore, is not necessarily bad.

Stress often is a powerful motivator and serves as a source for individual achievements. In a scientific sense, stress is Mother Nature's master-key in evolution. Every organism is provided with its own non-specific stress response to its changing environments, and its survival depends on how well the organism counters the stressor.

Stress, *per se,* is not harmful, but the inability to deal with it is. Stress does not kill, but the stress-induced ailment can. It happens when the stress moves from the psyche-plane (mind) to the somatic-plane (body). That is, the effects of prolonged stress begin to manifest as organic diseases, commonly known as psychosomatic illnesses. We will be seeing more about stress in Part 2. Needless to say, the more we learn about stress, the easier it is managed preventively and creatively.

The Road Ahead—
Life is to live and not to lament

Living is looking forward towards the unknown horizon with the willingness to look at the surrounding realities of life, however pleasant or unpleasant they may seem to be. What is at the horizon? Who knows? It is no different from the beautiful rainbow adorning the blue sky, making you wonder at its uncertain existence. Enjoy it while it lasts, and store it in your memory. In the same way, your life's horizon is beyond your reach. You have no choice but to move towards it step by step, one day at a time. The key, then, is to live each day well, at the same time keeping an eye on the horizon. Today is the tomorrow you had been dreaming about yesterday.

What is living well? Each person may have a different answer, but you will agree with me when I say that living well implies living to the fulfillment of our desires, ambitions and aims. **Hans Selye** calls it *the fulfillment of the need for self-expression,* which he considers as the ultimate aim of man, the individual.

Also, living well implies that one does not waste one's valuable "adaptation energy" lamenting over past mishaps and unpleasant life-events. Feeling guilty and blaming oneself for the occurrence, without any attempt to accept or alter the stressful situation or throwing the blame on others, breeds only more stress, whose effects are bound to be devastating in the long run.

A little reflection will point out that our road ahead should lead us to the conservation of our adaptation energy and, at the same time, make it possible for us to live a life of satisfaction and self-fulfillment.

For the individual to lead a meaningful life and to make the most out of it, he or she must understand oneself first, and then others as people having their own individuality. Understanding this is important in preventing or minimizing the stressors in interpersonal relationship and letting the individual develop his or her potentials for self-expression.

Secondary Evolution—
The least understood phenomenon

From birth to death man is constantly undergoing a secondary process of evolution through the interplay between his mental and bodily reactions and his adaptation to his environment or the society where he lives. Successful adaptation brings him health and happiness while failure to do so leaves him sick in body and unhappy in mind. Man has it in his power to influence this secondary evolution to a considerable extent, and as **Selye** emphasized "especially if he understands its mechanism and has enough will power to act according to the dictates of human intellect."

Alas! The adaptation to the stresses and strains of everyday existence is not as easy as it sounds. Let us take a casual look around us. It is almost unbelievable that in this richest nation on earth, millions suffer from nervous and emotional disturbances, high blood pressure, gastric and duodenal ulcers, cardiovascular and renal diseases, which are branded by the medical science as *diseases of adaptation* or simply as stress-induced ailments.

Concept of Self and Stress

The secondary evolution of the individual is purely a subjective phenomenon. It is set into motion from the instant the "self-consciousness" is born in the individual at a very early childhood, when the child becomes aware of its "I" being distinct and different from others in its needs and existence. This "I" stays with the individual till death. From the very beginning the "I" or "ego" occupies the center stage of the individual's life—directing, controlling, and influencing his or her every conscious action. This gives rise to the first law of behavioral psychology—that all human beings act at their own self-interest.

The body-mind partnership of the "I" concept is unique for each individual. In a subjective sense, each person has his or her own "self-image". Whenever this self-image has difficulty in adapting to a given change of environment or a stressor, the person experiences stress.

The fact that different people react differently to a given stressor shows that the mind behind the "I" concept is different in each person and that the self-image founded on the constituents of the mind is also different. The inference is that a stressor induces stress in some minds and not in others.

Of course, this is an interesting and intriguing phenomenon, but it is not just an academic interest. Herein lies the key for preventive stress management. To subjectively try to make suitable alterations in our mental "make-up" and "self-image" is the most logical step in our quest for stress management.

It is futile to hope that stress will go away by itself, for it will not, as long as the stressor persists. Effort on your part towards successful adaptation to the stressor is required.

Homeostasis and Equanimity

What kind of effort is required? This precisely is the subject matter of this book. The effort is in the direction of your body-mind partnership. It is aimed at the homeostasis of the body and equanimity of the mind. *Homeostasis* is the body's tendency to maintain its physiologic stability despite external changes. *Equanimity* is the emotional balance under stressful conditions. It simply means that your effort is needed in influencing your own secondary evolution, and you must be aware that it is a continuing process involving the transformation of your self-image to a new "I" capable of successful adaptation to life's challenges.

The Meaning of Self-Excellence

The totality of the body-mind improvement is expressed in one term, "self-excellence." There is more in this term than what meets the eye. Excellence of the body is easily understood as a healthy and vibrant physique, free from aches and pains, muscle tensions and diseases—the kind of physique that everyone desires to have. However, excellence of the mind, expressing equanimity, is not that easy to comprehend. From a stress management point of view, it is a reflection of the self-image which is capable of meeting the challenges of life and dealing with it constructively. You may call it a confident and positive self-image. What steps can one take to improve or build a better self-image which is nurtured and sustained by the mind of the individual? In other words, the question is how to improve the mind, using the mind itself. It is a paradox. Modern psychology is yet to find its way out of this.

Leaving the paradox to the psychologists, let us take a look at the human body and mind the way the great philosophers of the East did five thousand years ago. Why? Because they had found a practical way to self-excellence and showed a path for stress-free living. The fact that their approach to life and their pragmatic methods formed the strong undercurrent of the Eastern cultures and that these cultures not only survived but also flourished over the millennia is reason enough for us to explore new grounds in our search for methods to conquer stress.

Chapter 2

The Triumph of Self-Excellence Over Stress

> "But in order for man to relate freely there must be something in him that is free to relate, something separate from or independent of the body. This independent "something" is precisely that consciousness which is spoken of in the perennial teachings, and precisely that which unperfected man lacks."
>
> **Jacob Needleman**
> Author of *A Sense of the Cosmos*

Man's attempt to conquer misery (stress in today's term) dates back to 5000 years. India's *Vedas* and *Upanishads,* the most ancient living scriptures of the world, deal with the way to live for health and happiness. Chinese and Japanese cultures abound in the methods to adore Nature and live in harmony with it. A whole new religion *Buddhism* arose from one man's search for the conquest of misery on earth.

Are there ideas from these ancient cultures that are relevent to our discussion on stress management under present day living conditions? Yes. They are found in the way their philosophers looked at the human life on earth and its relation to the Universe. Let us briefly review them to get a proper perspective of our own problems.

Man the Microcosm and the Universe the Macrocosm

Man is considered as a part of the whole which is the living Universe, the cosmos. The Universe is characterized by unchanging eternal nature's laws. These laws provide the three main attributes of the cosmos, *order, balance and harmony.* The awesome and infinite magnitude of the power of the forces of the cosmos is beyond the intellectual comprehension of the human being, whose very existence depends on the mercy of these forces. Man himself, along with all that exists on this earth and in this Universe, animate and inanimate, has come into existence through the conscious interplay of the cosmic forces through the stages of a cosmic evolution. This cosmic evolution is not a mechanical process, but it is consciousness-directed and purposive. Hence, all the forces of nature are in man's physical body, and all the elements of the body possess inherently the three cosmic attributes—order, balance and harmony. (In modern medical language they are called homeostasis).

Because man is a true reflection of the living cosmos, he is known as the microcosm. He is, in fact, a part of the total, which is called the Universe or macrocosm. Microcosmic man is eternally bound to the macrocosmic universe, and as such he does not have an independent existence of his own. The cosmic connection is his breathing, which provides him with cosmic sustenance for his mortal body through the life-energy derived from the very cosmos itself.

The Human Body as a Path

The human being is considered to have a physical body and a mind, linked by the life-energy. The body, having evolved from the interplay of cosmic forces, is basically pure. It is governed by nature's laws (cosmic laws) of birth, growth, decay and death. The indweller of this body is the cosmic energy, "I", which is not the body. "I" is the individualized cosmic consciousness.

Pursuit of the pleasures of the flesh is not the purpose of the body. However, sensual enjoyment is not prohibited. It is regulated for procreation and for bodily health. It is the duty of the individual to take care of his or her body with the utmost care and use it as a path towards mental purification and cosmic realization.

The Human Mind

The human mind is considered to have four sheaths or elements:
    emotion
    creativity
    intellect
    intuition.

Anger, fear, grief and joy are considered to be the four fundamental or basic emotions, and their combinations give rise to multitudinous shades of human feelings. Emotions arise due to "I" consciousness of the individual when the person identifies himself with the mortal physical body. This is the "ego" state of the individual.

The "individuality" of the person is no more different from the "individuality" of a droplet of water of the ocean splashed up in the air separated from the wave which breaks into myriads of droplets. The person as an individual has in him or her as much attributes of the cosmic background as the droplet has in it those of the ocean.

It is "ego", the false identity, that lies at the base of all human misery. So long as the cosmic identity of the person is not realized, the "ego" consciousness persists, and the emotions burst out at the assertation of "I", "my" and "mine" through bodily expressions of words and actions. All learning is directed towards the taming of the emotions through intellectual effort and bringing the mind to a state of serenity, known as "equanimity".

Creativity is a fundamental element of the mind in all human beings. Unlimited potential for creativity and learning is dormant in the mind and is waiting to be released. It is derived from the creative forces inherent in the cosmos.

Intellect is the non-emotional reasoning power of the mind which has the ability to use logic and see through the cause and effect of the events of the phenomenal world. Intellect is at the source of all human knowledge related to life on earth. It serves as the discriminator of good and bad in thought, speech and action. Intellect is easily clouded by emotion, and a distortion of truth happens. Hence, strong emphasis is laid to hold the emotions at bay at all times.

Intuition or intuitive consciousness of the person is the knower of truth. It is the real "I" consciousness. It is also referred to as the "spirit" or "soul" of the individual. Intuition is totally submerged under the sheaths of emotion, creativity and intellect. It can be reached by transcending these three mental sheaths through meditation.

Pleasure Versus Happiness

The scriptures make a clear distinction between pleasure and happiness. Pleasure is sense-oriented and is enjoyed through the contact of the sensory organs for seeing, hearing, tasting, smelling and physical contact. It is short-lived and physical. On the other hand, happiness is a state of mind which does not depend on sensory input. Intellectual pursuits and meditation induce a state of euphoria and happiness. Meditation is the royal path to happiness.

Excess indulgence of physical pleasures lead to physical and mental pain. State of happiness has no such side effects. One person's pleasure can be the source of pain and anguish for another, whereas happiness is distinguished with absence of pain, mental or physical, in himself or others.

Pleasure is selfish. Happiness is sharing. The former is ego-centered, and places the self-interest ahead of others, whereas the latter is just the opposite and considers others first.

Purpose of Human Life

Every life has a purpose in living. Every being is an element in the tapestry of Nature. It adds color, hue and shade to its environment. The purpose of every human being is to realize his or her due place in the cosmic tapestry and adapt to the surrounding elements (people and place) in such a way that the creative and intellectual potentials are fully utilized to bring out the order, harmony, and balance in his or her life and to help to bring these potentials out in the lives of others with whom he or she is cast.

Uniqueness Characteristic of the Human Mind

There is a uniqueness characteristic in every human mind. It is this uniqueness that sets one person apart from another and imparts the human individuality. It is distinguishable by a uniquely different manifestation of the triple elements: emotion, creativity and intellect of the mind in each individual, though combined in an inseparable complexity, not amenable for analysis. This combination of the psychic energies is peculiar to the individual. The person functions at his best only when his actions are in tune with his psychological uniqueness.

But for this uniqueness characteristic, man would have been doomed to an animalistic existence of stereotyped behavior—everybody behaving the sameway as everybody else does. In some persons the emotional energy shows up overwhelmingly, in some the intellectual energy is predominant, and in others the creative energy is at its best.

The "knower" in the body (the individualized microcosmic "I") has the power to know the make-up of his or her own mind through equanimity. When a person's action is in tune with his uniqueness, he experiences a sense of joy and happiness (not pleasure) and feels the mental peace and serenity of which he becomes consciously aware. His mind will be in a state of equanimity.

On the contrary when the person's action is not in unison with his uniqueness, he experiences unhappiness and feelings of discomfort in his mind. The equanimity of his mind is disturbed, and he comes under the influence of his own emotions, displaying anger, fear, grief, or any combination thereof.

It is the sheer ignorance and the lack of disciplined effort on the part of man, the individual, to understand his own uniqueness, which acts as a dark screen thrown over his eyes blinding him to his intuitive, intellectual, and creative potentials.

Role of Individual Effort

According to the scriptures, life (that is, the process of living) is not fatalistic. The individual is provided with a body and mind with all the potentials for development through self-effort to cognize and work towards the purpose. It is akin to the individual being placed in a row-boat with food and water to last for a while and placed on the stream of life and left to his will. Destiny is in his hands to learn to row and steer the boat intelligently to a safe landing towards a self-determined goal on the shore with determination and self-effort, or to cry and wail his lot, letting the boat drift away to the ocean without taking any effort on his part.

Effort must be his own to dig out and know his potentials, to know his mission or purpose of living, and to move towards his goal. Effort must be his own to develop the health of the body and the faculties of the mind for harmonious blending or adaptation to the lives of people surrounding him, and at the same time holding his own.

The Power of Self-Excellence

The self-realized soul identifies itself with the eternal and infinite Cosmic Consciousness, whereas the unrealized soul identifies itself with the mortal body of finite existence. The self-realized person has crossed the pain-pleasure barrier in mundane living by virtue of disciplined cultivation of his or her body and mind to their full potentials. He (or she) enjoys his (or her) life on earth and contributes to enrich the lives of others. He (or she) has reached a state of self-excellence.

The unrealized person lives with a pleasure-seeking mission and is dominated by the emotions. His (or her) greed and selfishness breed the inevitable pain to the body and mind. He (or she) makes his (or her) life miserable and also those of others. His (or her) life becomes meaningful to him (or her) and to others only when the person moves towards a state of self-excellence.

It is at this point that we take leave of the scriptures of the East, and turn our attention to the realities of the modern-day living where stress is inevitable and to our quest for ways and means of preventive stress management.

5 Steps of Self-Excellence

The accumulated wisdom of the Eastern cultures has something to offer the individual for this successful adaptation to worldly living by way of time-tested techniques. These techniques have the power to quickly elevate him to a state of equanimity where he can bloom to his fullest innate potentials. They steer him towards self-excellence, physically and mentally, as he takes on a life of planned goals.

Self-excellence is a subjective and self-realized state of being as far as the individual is concerned. It is both a means and an end as it becomes a way of life for the individual culminating in unparalleled mental peace and inner happiness. Self-excellence is achieved through a 5-step process involving both the physical body and the conceptual mind, linked through a meditative feedback. The 5 steps are presented in detail in Part 4 of this book.

Validity of Self-Excellence in the Modern World

Of course, the world of today is not the same as the world of past centuries, and the value systems of our societies today are not the same as those of the bygone centuries either. However, two things remain the same: one is man's quest for health and happiness, and the other is his instinctive desire for excellence.

Excellence! How can one seek excellence outside of himself without first attempting to realize it within himself? Self-excellence in the modern world is nothing else but man's internal growth to meet the challenges and crises that confront him in the socio-economic milieu, successful adaptation to his cultural background and the development of his innate potentials of his body and mind to match the changes brought about by technology in the world around him.

Anthropologists and psychologists have observed that human beings have an inborn nature to strive for excellence as an element of adaptation. This is also true of all organisms in their struggle for survival. **The emergence of the beautiful butterfly from the clumsy caterpillar is but a glimpse of the innate excellence in evolution. However, only man has it in his power to move towards self-excellence using the power of his intellectual process in a conscious manner and bring about his , so-called, secondary evolution.**

He has the ability to self-realize through his brain and nervous system the inadequacies and shortcomings in his attitudes, knowledge and behavior with reference to his social and environmental stressors. The self-realization awakens in him the quest for ways and means of adaptation to the stressors and directs him toward self-excellence. This, then, is the solution to the stress problems of the modern man. More than ever self-excellence is needed for him today not only for survival but also to enjoy all fruits of the technological innovations and to create an external world of excellence—a better place to live in for all.

PART 2

All About Stress

Chapter 3

The Stress of Life

> "When the emotions of anger, fear, joy or sorrow are not stirred, the mind may be said to be in the state of equanimity. When those feelings have been stirred, and they act in their due degree, there ensues what may be called the state of harmony."
>
> **Confucius**
> 5th century Chinese saint and philosopher

Definition of Stress

The word stress means different things to different people. To the engineer who deals with the design, construction, and maintenance of structures and machines, it means a force per unit area. To the weatherman stress means the pressure conditions of the atmosphere. To the biologist it may mean the constrained conditions of cellular existence. To the sportsman it means the strained activity or exertion toward the accomplishment of his goal. To the stage actor or a speaker it means the intensity of utterance given to a syllable or word producing relative loudness. In normal usage the word stress is synonymous with strain, pressure, tension, shear, thrust, tortion, and emphasis.

Webster defines stress as a physical, chemical or emotional factor (as a trauma, histamine or fear) to which an individual fails to make a satisfactory adaptation, and which causes physiologic tensions that may be a contributive cause of disease.

However, in the last few decades stress has become a household word meaning an emotional stress, ever since **Dr. Hans Selye** formulated his revolutionary concept of stress, which opened up countless new avenues of treatment through the discovery that hormones participate in the development of many nonendocrine degenerative diseases, including coronary thrombosis, brain hemorrhage, hardening of the arteries, certain types of high blood pressure and kidney failures, arthritis, peptic ulcers, and even cancer. According to **Selye,** stress is "a state manifested by a syndrome." Though stress shows itself as a specific syndrome, it is non-specifically induced. The stress syndrome consists of all the non-specifically induced changes in the body at any one time.

Anything that produces a state of stress is referred to as a stressor. The stressor may be transcient, or it may last for a longer period of time. The sum of all the non-specific changes as they develop throughout time during continued exposure to a stress is called the general adaptation syndrome (or G.A.S.).

It may be noted that both the stressor and the body's response to it are often called by the same term, stress.

Subjective Nature of Stress

Stress is purely a subjective phenomenon. What causes severe stress to one person may affect only lightly another person. For example, the death of a person beloved to an individual may cause intense stress to the later, but may be of light grief to a casual neighbor. It is this element of emotion associated with stress, which constitutes the core of human existence and the pursuit of pleasure and happiness in mundane living. Stress and its effects on our emotions will be discussed elsewhere in this book.

Since stress is a subjective occurrence, prevention or management of stress also becomes subjective in the sense that the individual can help himself or herself to a great degree by learning what to do and what not to do with reference to potential stressors. It is the primary objective of this book to help the reader to help himself or herself in the art and science of preventive stress management and creative living.

Seven Universal Laws of Stress

Stress is inevitable in life. It is normal and natural to feel stressed in the course of daily living. Stress in itself is neither bad nor good. What is important is your response to it and your ability to manage it; or simply, it is your ability to adapt to the rigors of the stressor.

Occurrence of stress in a person is universal. By knowing under what circumstances stress occurs, one will be able to manage or

prevent the stress more effectively than otherwise. Based on subjective psychology, the following are the seven universal laws of stress:
1. Stress occurs when changes take place in the physiological or psychological equilibrium.
2. Stress occurs when survival is threatened. The threat may be real or imagined.
3. Stress occurs when self-image is threatened. The threat may be real or imagined.
4. Stress occurs when there is an unresolved conflict in the conscious or subconscious level of mind.
5. Stress occurs when a desired goal becomes elusive and unattainable.
6. Stress occurs when personal loss is encountered. The loss may be real or imagined.
7. Stress occurs when deadlines are encountered.

These seven laws of stress constitute the fundamental understanding of stress for anyone desiring to cope with it. The possible sources of stress are discussed in a later chapter. It must be held in view that while the laws of stress are universal in nature, the sources of stress can be selective in that a given source of stress may affect only selective personalitites.

Signs of Stress in a Person

Though non-specific in nature, prolonged stress can induce specific bodily responses and psychosomatic ailments. The readily observable signs and symptoms in a person under prolonged stress are:
1. Loss of, or disturbed, sleep
2. Headache
3. Overuse of coffee, tea, cigarettes, drugs, food, and alcohol
4. Onset of stomach ulcer
5. Display of chronic impatience
6. Display of chronic temper
7. Onset of prediabetic condition (increased blood sugar level above normal)
8. Display of despondency and grief (depression and a sense of hopelessness)
9. Loss of interest in career, family, and life in general.

It may be noted here that the above signs and symptoms are deviations from equanimity of the mind, homeostasis of the body, and enthusiasm in living which are the very antithesis of self-excellence. Removal of them implies the restoration of self-excellence.

Stress in Daily Life

Stress and modern living go hand in glove. Ours is a fast changing world. From the slow pace of living at the turn of the last century the present era has dawned into a fast moving technologically oriented way of living where the traditional cultural, religious, and social values are fastly losing their ground. Unable to comprehend the change many among us are swept off our feet and are drifting in the current of life with no specific goals and directions. As a result, we are confronted with many conflicts within ourselves and with the world we live in.

Even those who seem to hold their ground and lead a materially comfortable life are often tormented by the changing value system of the world around and are pushed to the extremes of emotions resulting in their mental unrest and unhappiness.

Striving for unrealistic achievements in an environment of unhealthy competition takes a heavy toll on the individual's mental and physical health. In the wake of spiralling inflationary trend in the Nation's economic milieu, the need to take a job and stay in it has increased for many individuals. The fluctuating job market has ushered the blue and white collar workers into a new era of stress.

Stress and the Modern Woman

More and more women are now competing in the once male dominated skilled and unskilled areas of the job market. Many women are fastly climbing up the corporate leadership. The younger generation of women students is now getting trained literally in every field of science and technology. All these constitute a change in the traditional role of women in society. However, to many individuals the role poses a new kind of stress to comprehend and deal with.

Loneliness

Though longevity has increased for the average American aging person, the traditional family living has changed. Many older people have to learn a different life not accustomed to in their active years. Loneliness, in many cases has been observed to be the single most important stressor.

Stress and Success

Ours is a "success" conscious society. Since the success of an individual is, unfortunately as it were, measured in terms of a person's monetary assets, the type of house one lives in, the type of car one drives, the power of office held, and the attraction to the opposite sex, the individual is constantly struggling, consciously or subconsciously, towards unrealistic goals. Those who have achieved a reasonable degree of the so-called "success" still have to struggle so they don't lose it, and those who are pushing themselves to achieve the illusionary "success" are often dismayed, distressed and frustrated. These are the people who are highly vulnerable to stress-related illnesses.

Threat of War

This is an age of uncertainty. Political turmoils and international economic fluctuations conspicuously affect every nation, thereby affecting every individual. Threat of nuclear war is no longer an imagined one. Incidence of crime in the Nation's large cities constantly pose a stress to those who live there.

Divorce

The traditional value system of marriage as such is taking a severe beating and there is no dearth for statistics to clearly indicate the increase in broken homes, ironically enough at a time when the modern technology is delivering unprecedented material comforts and conveniences to be enjoyed at home.

There are numerous situations in day to day life which may invoke feelings of anxiety and frustrations, such as having to drive to and from work every day in heavy traffic, having to stomach unpleasant responses from an unfriendly boss, working in a job that one does not care for, repeated arguments with the spouse at home, the impending visit of a mother-in-law and the constant lurking pressure to keep up with the Joneses next door. Psychologists point out that whatever is the provoking situation the direct consequence of the feelings of frustrations is stress in the mind of the individual.

From the foregoing discussion it is apparent that some form of stress is unavoidable in your daily life. The question then is what effect does stress have on the individual. It must be emphasized here that not all people react the same way when exposed to the same stressing situaion. This brings to focus the behavioral response of the individual. Varying responses are conceived and executed depending on the individual's mental makeup. Thus what appears as a serious situation to one, may be brushed off as a minor occurrence by another. A case in view is a rejection of a suitor by a lover. In the former the effect can be psychologically damaging, whereas in the later it may not have any significant impact at all.

Stress and Your Emotions

If stress is such an integral part of our living, then why should we be so much concerned about it? If stress does not interfere with your normal functioning physiologically and psychologically, then, of course, you can completely discount stress from your life as something of a routine occurrence. But, as it were, unfortunately, stress is directly related to your emotions and has the potential to affect your physical health. Every stressor is a potential emotion inducer. It may be anger, fear or grief, the intensity of which is dependent on the nature of the stressor and the psychological make-up of the individual. Hence, a good understanding of the physiological and psychological components of stress is a must when you aspire for relaxation and stress management.

Chapter **4**

Physiological Aspects of Stress

"The physiological machinery of behavior is exceedingly complex. In principle, however, it is simple."

Clifford T. Morgan
Author of *Physiological Psychology*

Emotions and the Endocrine Glands

How does the body respond to the emotions that arise or are provoked in the mind? Until about a century ago, the nervous system was generally considered as the one controlling force for the complex body processes. However, too many bodily phenomena appeared to have no relationship to the nervous system, and the missing link was then found in the endocrine glands. These are glands of internal secretion with no ducts or tubes. Their secretions go directly into the blood stream, and their effects are quickly felt in areas far away from the glands.

The substances they secrete are called hormones. They are powerful chemical regulators which control the size, shape and appearance of the body, influence your emotions and mental state, and ally with the nervous system in determining the kind of individual you are and controlling many of your body's functions.

Hypothalamus:
The Supreme Body-Mind Bridge

The location of the seven endocrine glands can be seen in Figure 1. The pituitary is considered the "leader" gland which secretes hormones to activate each of the other endocrine glands. The pituitary

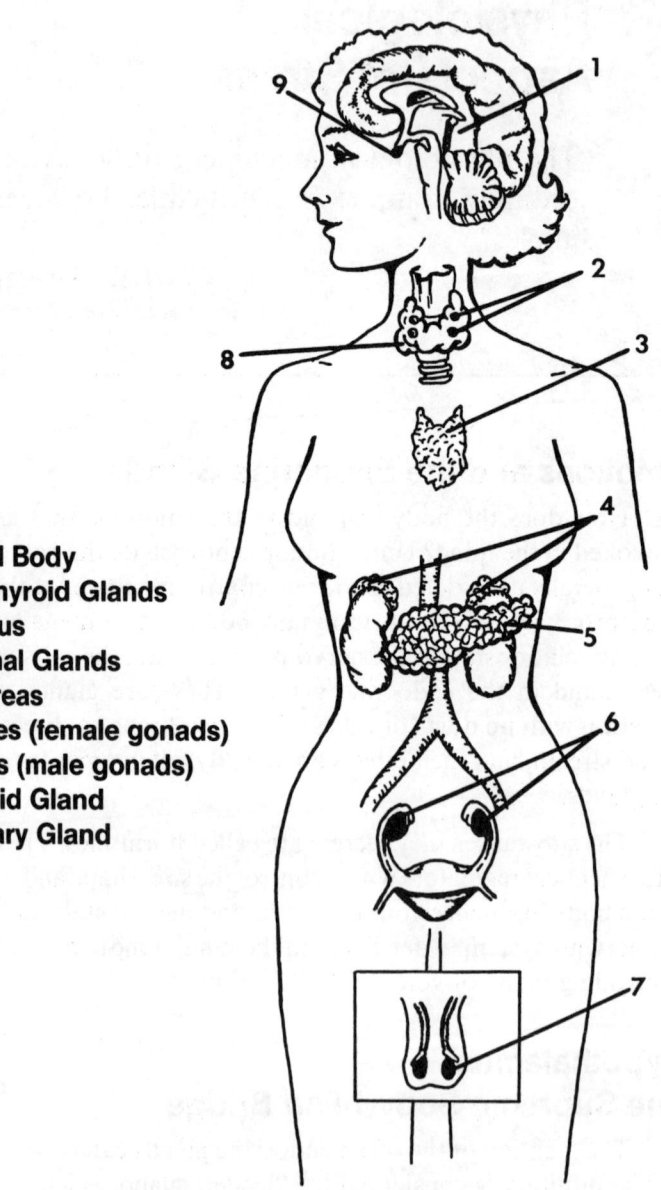

Figure 1. Endocrine system.

itself is "commanded" by a small lobe at the base of the brain, called the hypothalamus to which it is connected. The electrochemical activity of the hypothalamus is considered to be the bridge between the mind and the body. The hypothalamus is important to us because it plays a vital role in all relaxation methods.

The Stress Hormones

At times of stress, the adrenal glands in the endocrine system located on top of the kidneys are activated by the hormone secreted by the pituitary gland. The adrenal medulla produces two closely related hormones, called epinephrine, also known as adrenaline, and norepinephrine or noradrenaline. The output of these hormones is stepped up when you are struck with emotions of fear and anger, and also when you are excited. The immediate effect of these hormones is to stimulate the sympathetic nervous system which steps up the blood pressure, heart rate, breathing rate, metabolism and blood flow to the muscles preparing the body for physical action. Hence these hormones are appropriately called the stress hormones. Their role in the stress-related physiological ailments is presented later.

Stress and the Nervous System

Between the endocrine system and the nervous system, there exists a close two-way relationship. The nerve impulses influence the glands, and the glands, in turn, influence the nerves. They are excited into action through emotions experienced under stressful events. The onset of emotions stirs up electrochemical activity in the hypothalamus, and thus the complex physiological response or human behavior is set in motion.

How does the hypothalamus act on the body and control the behavior? The answer lies in the nervous system, which may be considered as two basic divisions—the central and the peripheral. The brain and the spinal cord constitute the central nervous system from which the cranial and the spinal nerves extend to all parts of the body. The peripheral nervous system is made up of all the nerves other than those in the brain and spinal cord. See Figure 2.

The central nervous system may be subdivided into two parts: the voluntary or skeletal nervous system and the involuntary or autonomic

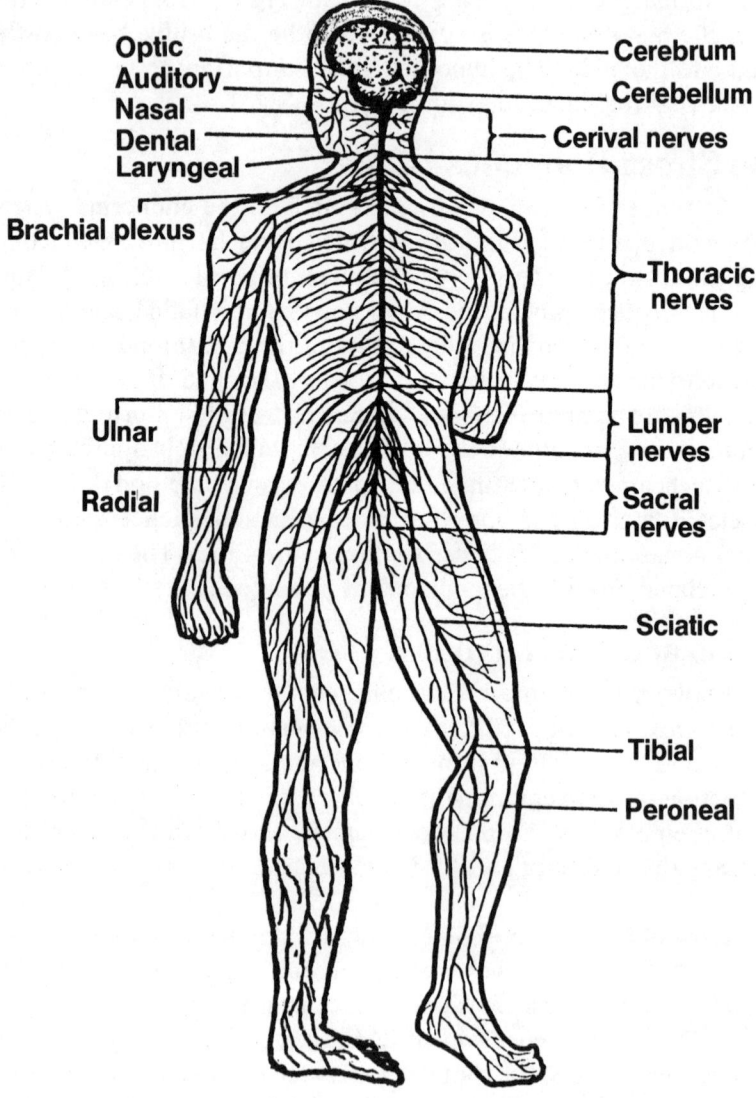

Figure 2. Central and peripheral nervous system.

PHYSIOLOGICAL ASPECTS OF STRESS

nervous system. When you desire to move your arms or legs, your brain sends message to them through the voluntary nervous system. The action is under your control at the conscious level of your mind. However, there are many bodily functions which do not come under your conscious control, such as heart beat, breathing, digestion of food, etc. They are controlled through your body's autonomic nervous system, controlled and regulated by the hypothalamus.

Sympathetic and Parasympathetic Nervous System

The autonomic nervous system, in turn, is divided into sympathetic and parasympathetic divisions. The two divisions usually operate in opposition to one another. For example, the sympathetic system speeds breathing while the parasympathetic slows it down, maintaining a precise balance. The former dilates the pupil of the eye, speeds up heart beat, constricts blood vessels and raises blood pressure, whereas the later constricts the pupil, slows down the heart beat, dilates the blood vessels and lowers the blood pressure.

The sympathetic nervous system starts at the base of the brain and runs along both sides of the spinal column. The nerves of this system reach glands such as salivary, sweat, liver and pancreas, and to muscles such as those in the iris of the eyes, stomach, heart, intestines and bladder. The walls of blood vessels are also connected by these nerves.

On the other hand, the parasympathetic system consists of two major nerves. One of them starts from the base of the brain stem and sends branches through the chest and abdomen. The other takes off from the spinal cord in the area of the hip and branches off to organs in the lower part of the body, including the kidneys and bladder. See Figure 3.

It is important that you have an understanding of these body biomechanisms, which will help you in effectively handling your stresses in everyday life. We may summarize by saying that the response to stress is carried out by the sympathetic nervous system and the relaxation counterpart is carried out by the parasympathetic nerves. Both of these systems are under the control of the hypothalamus.

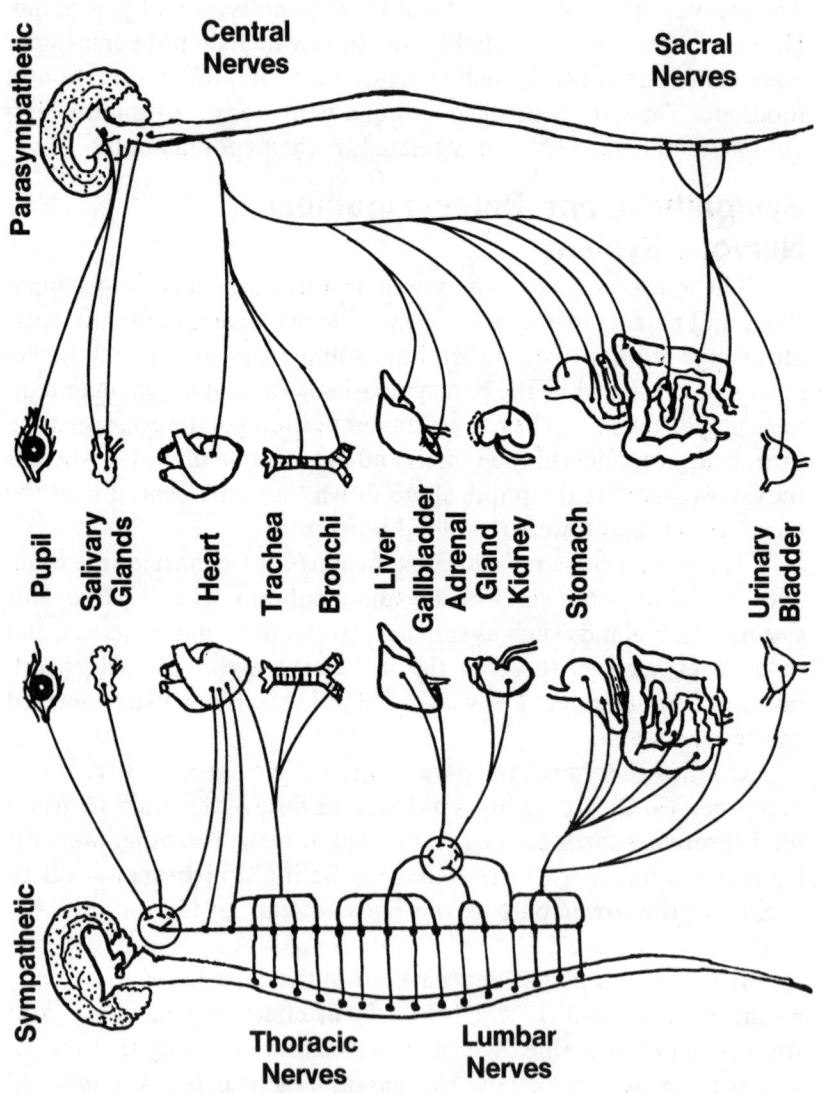

Figure 3. Autonomic nervous system.

Brain, Hypothalamus and Stress

The brain, at the anterior end of the spinal cord, is the largest and the most complex part of the nervous system. It functions as the control center for the entire nervous system. It interprets the signals from the sense organs, guides our movements, holds the memory and enables us to think. Basically, the brain may be considered to consist of three parts: the forebrain including the cerebrum, the thalamus and the hypothalamus, the midbrain including the reticular core and the hindbrain consisting of the brain stem, the cerebellum, the medulla and the pons (Figure 4).

The hypothalamus is considered as the neurocenter of the brain which controls and regulates the sympathetic and parasympathetic divisions of the nervous system. Neurologists, physiologists and psychologists agree that the hypothalamus is the most important center from the point of view of homeostasis and emotions for it is here that the autonomic control is integrated. And, it is in the hypothalamus where our responses to stress originate. We had mentioned before about its influence over the endocrine system and the production of stress hormones by the adrenal glands at times of stress. The hypothalamus also regulates our thirst and hunger.

Stress and Brain Waves

The state of an individual such as in sleep or in activity has been studied extensively through the electrical impulses produced by the brain, commonly known as brain waves. Electrodes are placed on the scalp and the amplified electrical impulses are recorded in an instrument called an encephalograph. The recorded brain wave, an electroencephalogram (EEG), is a series of wavy lines which can be interpreted in terms of its occurence in frequencies every second, referred to as hertz(hz).

An alert and physiological activity produces brain impulses in the range of 13 to 30 hertz. These are called beta waves. The impulses during a state of rest of a person who is awake but with eyes closed and not unduly excited mentally are in the range of 8 to 13 hertz, and are known as alpha waves. At a semi-sleep state the brain produces waves at a range from 4 to 7 hertz, which are known as theta waves. Waves of

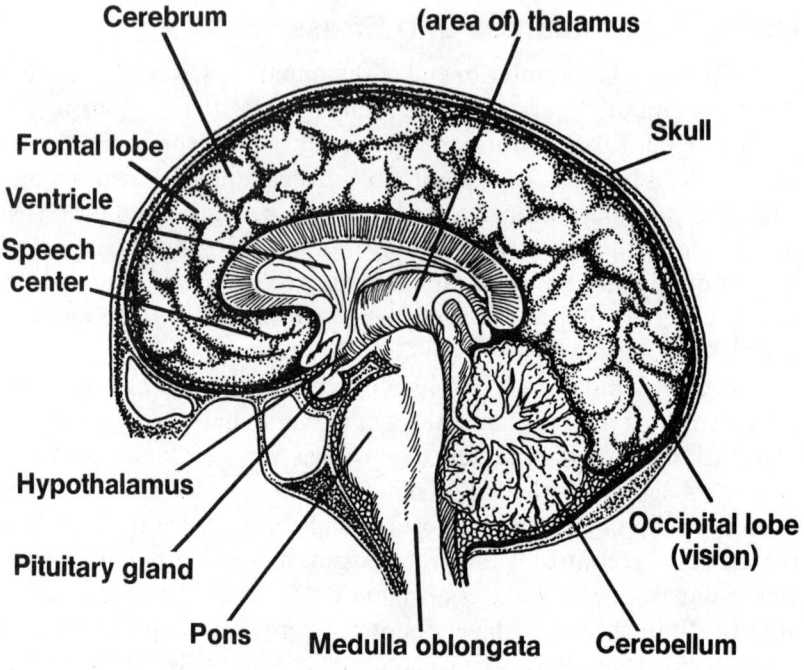
Figure 4. The brain.

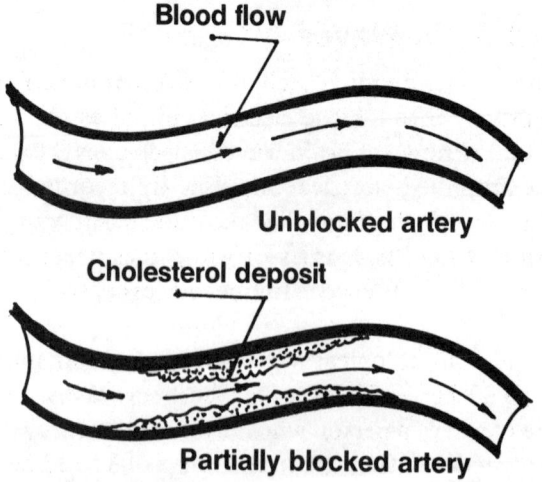
Figure 5. Unblocked and partially blocked arteries.

very low frequency, fewer than 4 per second, occur during deep sleep and are known as delta waves.

We will learn more about brain waves later in our discussion on relaxation elsewhere in this book. However, it should be pointed out here that your state of emotional arousal under stressful situations kindles electrochemical activity in your hypothalamus. This pushes up the brain wave frequency into the beta region, whereas relaxation of the body and mind calms down the hypothalamus to produce waves of alpha, theta or delta regions.

Stress and the Fight or Flight Response

In the process of daily living you are likely to go through different emotional experiences, some of them pleasant and some unpleasant. It is the unpleasant ones that we are mainly concerned about because they have the potential to induce stress. When the unpleasant emotions are well-managed, they leave no residual distress on the body or mind. But, what happens if you are swung to an extreme of an emotion under a stress producing situation, such as an intense anger or fear?

Let us answer this question by examining a hypothetical situation in which you come face to face with a ferocious angry dog, manifesting its bared teeth which has poised itself to attack you in fury.

Your mind senses the potential threat to your safety and survival, and a sense of intense fear grips you which paralyses you momentarily. The rational thinking process in you is taken over by the instinct for survival which sees only two options- one to face the dog and fight it, and the other to run away to safety from the source of threat.

Faced with a similar threat all bioorganisms behave predictably and precisely in the same manner of getting ready to fight or run away. This is an instinctual response which has helped organisms to survive over perhaps millions of years. **Dr. Walter Cannon** of the Harvard Medical School described this as the "emergency response", now popularly known as the "fight or flight" response.

Instantly the autonomic nervous system is stimulated and the body undergoes marked physiological changes. The hypothalamus activates the pituitary gland. This, in turn, activates the adrenal glands. The adrenal medulla secretes hormones adrenaline and noradrenaline, and the adrenal cortex secretes hydrocortisone and aldosterone into the blood stream. The immediate effect of the release of these hormones is manifested physiologically by increases in blood pressure, heart beat rate, rate of breathing, muscular tension, metabolism and blood flow to the muscles preparing the body for an encounter or escape. The stress hormones can also bring about increased platelet clumping in the blood and coronary artery spasm. The hormone adrenaline acts on the liver where sugar is stored as animal starch, called glycogen. The released glycogen gets into the blood stream as glucose, increasing its sugar content which provides the extra energy needed for the muscles.

The other stress hormone noradrenaline acts on the fat, stored as neutral fat under the skin and other parts of the body, and mobilizes these fat reserves by splitting the neutral fat into free fatty acids and glycerol, which then pass out of the fat cell into the blood stream. The free fatty acids can be used as a source of fuel by any muscle of the body, including the heart.

Now returning to our question what happens to the body when faced with an extreme emotion provoking situation, you can visualize the chain of physiological changes that take place once the fight or flight response is evoked. Assuming that you had a successful encounter with the dog or that you ran away to safety, the excess energy mobilized in your blood stream in the form of sugar and free fatty acids would have been consumed by the muscle actions in the process. The sugar level in your blood stream would thus return to the normal level maintained by your body's homeostatic mechanism. The free fatty acids in the blood, having been fully spent, would be eliminated as body wastes through urine and sweat.

Of course, you would feel exhausted and physically drained after the ordeal. The entire process is, in fact, an adaptation technique devised by Nature to a stressful situation, originally called the "general adaptation syndrome" by **Selye**.

Stress, Emotion and High Blood Pressure

In the modern so-called "civilized" living, you are inhibited to fight or run away from stressful situations, and you try other means to cope with them. However angry you are at your boss, spouse or neighbor, you can not physically fight them out; you can not run away from a traffic block when you are late for an important appointment. You can not help stomaching your anxieties and frustrations, and at the same time trying to "grin and bear it". Nevertheless, in all such cases of stress, the fight or flight response is elicited in varying degrees with the immediate stimulation of the autonomic nervous system and the consequent chain actions with the secretion of the stress hormones from the adrenal glands into the blood stream. The net result is an increased sugar and fat content in the blood, since they were not utilized in the absence of the fight or flight for which they were intended.

Of course, an isolated incidence of an "emotion stomaching" is not going to start hypertension (high blood pressure) overnight. But when your life style, habits, and attitudes are such as to elicit the fight or flight response often enough to become chronic, then you are a sure candidate for the development of high blood pressure, and related heart, brain and kidney ailments.

Stress and Cholesterol

Few people are aware of the influence of stress on the cholesterol level in the blood, though many are well informed about the undesirability of excess cholesterol in the blood serum, which has been found associated with high blood pressure and arterial hardening problems. We mentioned before that if the fight or flight response is aroused too often, and if the energy mobilized by the stress hormones are not utilized by the muscles, then the blood chemistry remains in a state of imbalance with an excess of metabolized sugar and neutral fat in the form of glycerol and free fatty acids.

This excess of free fatty acids and the glycerol unused in muscle activity tend to combine back chemically to form fat and cholesterol, which, over a long period of time, gets deposited on the walls of the blood vessels.

Stress and Atherosclerosis (Hardening of the Arteries)

As you grow older the arterial walls harden and thicken, losing their elasticity. The elasticity can also be lost due to slow deposition of the free fatty acids and cholesterol which are excessively present in the blood stream due to reasons of stress and a high intake of cholesterol-rich food. The net result is to adversely affect the dilating ability or the elastic rebound of the arteries on one hand, and to reduce the inside diameter of the blood flow path on the other. These deposits are also referred to as plaque which may be likened to the formation of rust on the inside walls of a pipe (Figure 5). Because of the narrowed flow path in the blood vessels, the heart is forced to pump more vigorously than before when the flow path was smooth and wider. This places additional strain on the heart muscles.

Stress and Artery Spasm

Dean Ornish from the Harvard Medical School points out in his book, *Stress, Diet and Your Heart,* that recent advances in diagnostic techniques used to examine living hearts have led to identify two other mechanisms that tend to reduce blood flow to the heart. One of them is coronary artery spasm and the other is platelet clumping in the artery.

Like all arteries, the coronary arterial wall is made up of elastic tissues and muscle fibers which make the artery elastic and resilient. We mentioned before that during times of stress the hypothalamus in your brain stimulates the sympathetic nervous system and activates the fight or flight response. This, in turn, activates the adrenal glands located on top of the kidneys which release the stress hormones adrenaline and noradrenaline into the blood stream directly. The blood enriched with the stress hormones reaches the heart quickly by the accelerated circulation. On the heart and in the coronary artery are located two types of adrenergic receptors. These are sensitive to the stress hormones secreted by the adrenal glands and are called the alpha and beta receptors. The alpha receptors are stimulated by the stress hormones present in the blood and also by small packets of adrenaline manufactured and stored in the nerve endings of the sympathetic nervous system located next to the alpha receptors. It is this stimulation of the alpha receptors that causes the constriction of the coronary arteries and causes the heart rate to increase.

On the other hand, the stimulation of the beta receptors causes the coronary arteries to dilate. It is believed that when the opposite conditions to that of stress prevail, such as total relaxation of the body and mind, the beta receptors are activated, dilating the arteries and slowing down the heart rate.

Stress and Sudden Death

It has been an unexplained phenomenon in the medical science for a long time until as late as a decade ago that normal healthy human beings have been found dead without any apparent cause. It has now come to light that intense emotional stress due to anger, fear, grief or even joy, can activate spasms in the coronary arteries. The arterial spasm interferes with the blood circulation, cutting off the blood supply to the heart and its muscles, which could lead to a possible sudden death.

Stress and Platelet Clumping

Blood platelets are minute, granular, disk-shaped objects in the blood which have their origin in the red marrow of the bone. They contain a number of chemical substances which make them stick together if there is an injury to the blood vessel and so are able to plug small breaks in capillaries. Obviously this ability of the blood to form a clot protects us from excessive bleeding from minor wounds and is Nature's gift to us for our survival.

Dr. Jacob Haft and fellow research workers discovered in the early seventies that under conditions of stress the platelets in the blood flowing in the arteries tend to stick together. They attributed this to the presence of the stress hormones adrenaline and noradrenaline in the blood which act as powerful stimulators on the platelets to clump. The clumped platelets release a thromboplastic chemical, which, in turn, induce more platelets to clump. Once formed the clumps tend to lodge on the walls of the arteries, obstructing the flow of blood.

Chapter 5

Psychological Aspects of Stress

"Although we live in a physical world, its meaning comes from our psychological view of it."

Philip G. Zimbardo
Author of *Psychology and Life*

Stress and Your Mind

The fact that the human being is a physiological entity endowed with a psyche, and at the same time has an individuality of his or her own while living in a social environment, makes it necessary for us to briefly discuss the human mind and its relationship to the body.

In order to understand and appreciate the human response to stresses arising during the course of daily living, stop for a minute, and ask yourself "Who am I? Why do I behave the way I do? Why am I under stress?"

The answers, of course, are not simple, but trying to contemplate on them will pave the way for a lucid understanding of life's problems and your reactions to them. The underlying causes of your stresses, anxieties and frustrations and their psychosomatic manifestations discussed elsewhere in this book can be traced to their very sources, and with this knowledge effective stress management will be a meaningful possibility.

"Mind" is a vague term. To this day it has defied all attempts for a precise definition by scholars and scientists. For all practical purposes we may consider mind as the non-matter counterpart of the brain, known as psyche. The mind is the subjective state of the individual whereas the body constitutes the organic state, and together they lend mutual support to provide the distinctness of the individual.

The Omega Effect

The British scientist, **G. R. Taylor,** in his book, *The Natural History of the Mind,* introduced the concept of the Omega Effect as the unique characteristic which will include our emotions, cognitive processes, subtle experiences, personal identity and consciousness. It is the Omega Effect that distinguishes man from a machine. Thus, the thoughts, feelings, sensations and perceptions of the individual can be considered to rest within the premises of the mind, making it possible to understand and analyze the human being as an individual identified by the body.

Subconscious Mind

Sigmund Freud, the founder of psychoanalysis, formulated the concept that human behavior can be explained in terms of the unconscious mind, the submergence of undesirable thoughts into it and the use of defense mechanisms to avoid recalling unpleasant experiences.

Motivations and Behavior

Human behavior arises from various motivations. Some of them have their roots in the biological drives of hunger, thirst, sex and sleep, while others are oriented towards basic human needs of safety, belongingness, self-esteem, creativity and curiosity to mention a few. Yet, all human beings are not motivated the same way, implying that there is a subtle difference in each human being in the manner in which he or she thinks, feels and acts.

Sense of Values of the Individual

What makes each person differ in their motivations can be traced to his or her value system or the sense of values of right and wrong and the concept of proper behavior. Psychologists refer to this as the personality traits. The personality formation is a continuous process starting from birth. The major contributing factors are cultural, social and religious environments in which one is raised.

As a child grows older, he is exposed to new experiences which are weighed in his mental scale against the values he has picked up and stored in the memory. This provides a feedback to make adjustments to his original values. However, he may feel guilty if his behavior violated his own sense of values at that time, and it could become an emotional experience.

Conflict in the Mind

Behavior is a dynamic, changing force throughout an individual's life in all its phases from infancy to old age, during which time one encounters many emotional situations. Most of them are resolved by accepting and adapting to the changes demanded by the situation. However, the ones which the individual could not accept and modify his behavior, crystallize into emotional conflicts. They may stay at the conscious level of the mind or sink to the unconscious. It is here **Freud's** psychoanalysis concept makes the greatest impact on the Science of Psychology as both a theory of personality and a method of treating personality disorders.

The emotional conflicts, no matter what they are due to, produce psychological discomfort and are the sources of stress. It is important for you to recognize this fact that behind every stress is an unresolved conflict whose physiological and psychological impacts are bound to follow.

Mechanism of Stress Response

Once encountered with a stressor, psychological and physiological responses are induced simultaneously, which are shown schematically in Figure 6.

Let us first consider the psychological aspect of the stressor. The information or input received by the hypothalamus of the brain through the sense organs is weighed, analyzed, and compared with the stored value system or the sense of values of the person, which we mentioned earlier. The emotions appear, and conflict, if any, is recognized. The input and the conflict are now placed on the short term memory of the brain. Eventually through a system of selective filters in the brain, they are recorded in the long term memory as an emotional experience which can be retrieved by the brain's feedback system later when desired.

Now, let us consider the physiological aspects of the stressor. With the onset of emotions (Omega Effect), the sympathetic branch of

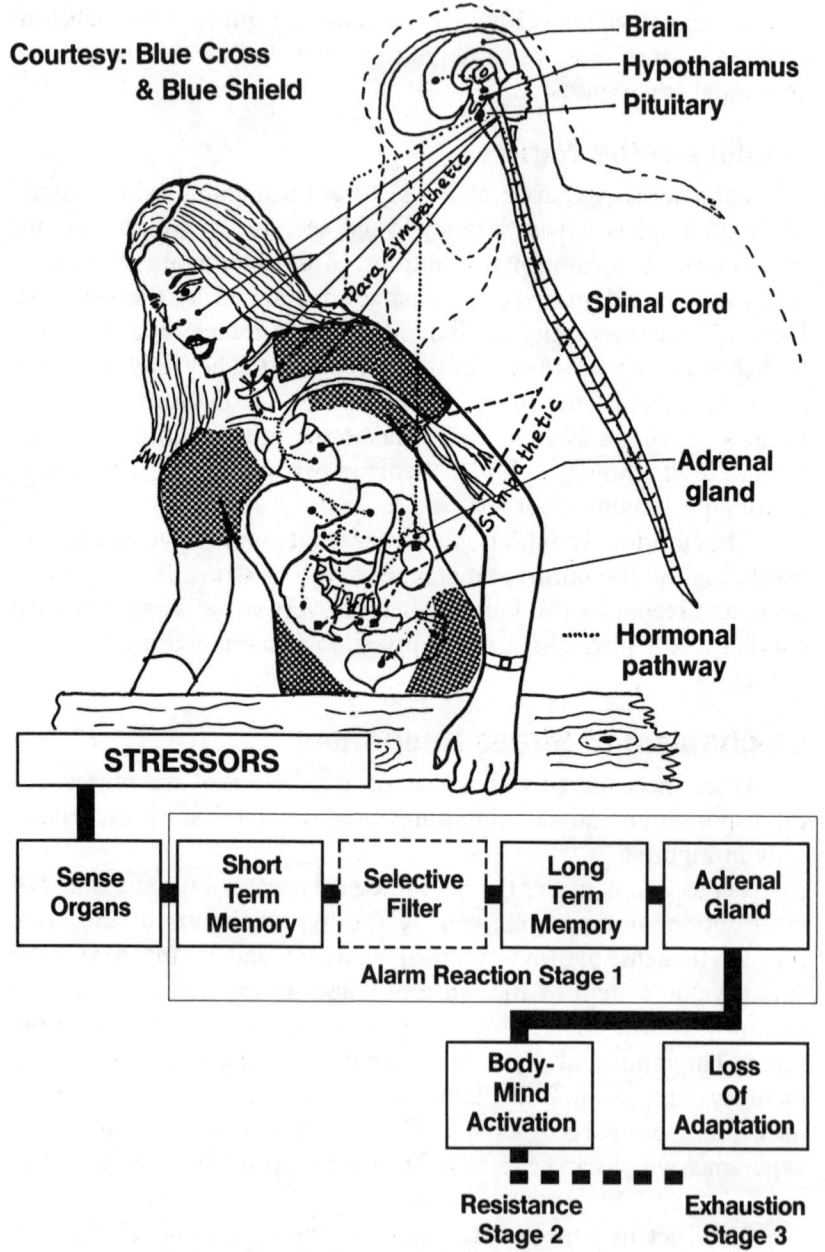

Figure 6. Psychophysiological stress response.

the autonomic nervous system takes over, which sounds an alarm reaction. This is the first stage when the heart rate and blood pressure rise up. A second stage of stress resistance follows by the activation of the adrenal gland which secretes the two types of hormones, adrenaline and noradrenaline, into the blood stream to facilitate the surging energy needed for the muscles for a fight or flight appropriate for the occasion. This is followed by the third stage of exhaustion when the body's defense system, upon being pushed for too long a time, loses its adaptation characteristics. The person is physically and mentally spent and feels tired. **Selye** called these three stages put together as the "general adaptation syndrome" or G.A.S.

Individuality and the Stress Reaction

Everyone does not respond to a given stressor to the same degree because of the individuality in personality which we had discussed before. The individual level of frustration tolerance, the intensity of the conflict producing situation and the cognitive reaction are the major factors in the varying stress response.

Stress and Your Emotions

Emotion is a feeling state accompanied by motor and glandular activity. Anger, fear, joy and sorrow are considered to be the four basic emotions. It is generally believed that the limbic system of the brain generates emotional response as an adaptive process for the survival of the organism.

Joy and the related terms happiness, delight and love are classified as pleasant emotions, whereas anger, fear and sorrow and their related states are classified as unpleasant. The pleasant emotions make us feel good and contribute positively for the physical and mental well-being of a person. They also help sustain the very living process and ensure the propagation of the species.

On the other hand, the unpleasant emotions make us feel bad and uncomfortable, and they have the potential to change the blood chemistry, disturbing the homeostasis of the body through the three stages of stress response mentioned earlier.

Frustration and Stress

Everyone experiences frustration at one time or another, be it a child or an older person. Interrupted or unaccomplished activities which a person has set oneself to complete induces frustration. It can be a simple transportation problem of reaching the office on time through heavy traffic or trying to complete the building of a house under tight financial restriction. It may be the case of a multi-million dollar corporation executive trying to put through an attractive but elusive deal on which his promotion rests. The case of a housewife trying to finish all the accumulated ironing before getting ready to pick up the children from school is not any different from the others mentioned.

The common element in all these cases is trying to "beat the deadline". In our present way of living, the clock on the one hand and the pressure to achieve on the other, constitute the potential for frustration in everyone's life. Frustration develops when you are are blocked or thwarted from progressing toward a predetermined goal. Regardless of its source, frustration is an uncomfortable, unpleasant and disturbing experience. Though it is considered as the consequence of a stressor, frustration acts on the mind producing discomfort and a state of tension.

The degree of susceptibility of people to frustration varies widely and is associated with what the psychologists call the frustration tolerance. Persons of low frustration tolerance are easily affected by stress, whereas those with a high tolerance level can withstand a great deal of stress.

Minor frustrations are normal human reactions and are not harmful to the well-being of a person. However, highly frustrated persons tend to become chronically very tense if the frustration persists over a long time. They may develop stress-related ailments, such as peptic ulcer, high blood pressure, asthma, skin rashes and migraine headaches to mention a few.

Anxiety and Stress

Anxiety is a feeling of overall tension resulting from a stress producing event or a situation. Whereas fear is a reaction to a specific threat, anxiety is an emotional response that is vague and undefined. It may be summed up as a fear of the unknown.

What is it that is threatened to cause psychological discomfort? It is the threat to the individual's value system or self-perception. The self-image of a person is the way one views himself which has evolved from his past experiences, learning and the sense of values he acquires through his socio-cultural environments. His value system also comprises his concept of his relations with other persons, his so-called self-prestige and views about the society he lives in. Anxiety sets in when these values are threatened and when he is unable to objectify these values.

Level of Anxiety

Anxiety is a normal reaction when it is dealt with at the conscious level and is proportionate to the stressing situation. However, since it is highly subjective in nature, there is a marked variation from person to person in his or her response to anxiety. Take the case of Jane who suffered severe headaches everyday for about a week prior to her mother-in-law's proposed visit. Her headache was completely gone when she learned that the mother-in-law cancelled her visit. The boy or girl getting ready for the first date and the applicant interviewing for a job that he is badly in need of are but cases of people in typical situations that provoke anxiety, the level of which is dependent on their personalities.

Anxiety Neurosis

Freud found that when the anxiety was not dealt with at the conscious level by willingly going through the stress producing situation, it is repressed into the unconscious and neurotic methods of avoiding the anxiety occurs. He describes the case of a young girl who suffered repeated nervous attacks marked by dizziness, buzzing in the ears, a crushing sensation in the chest, constriction of the throat and sensations of impending death, which he attributed to repressed anxiety. The organic discomforts vanished when he was able to point out to her the source of anxiety after a thorough psychoanalytic examination.

The repressed anxiety stays as a conflict in the unconscious and may reappear in various forms such as a neurosis, psychosis, subliminal behavior or psychosomatic disturbance. The associated physiological responses well documented in the medical literature are bulimia (excessive appetite), peptic ulcer, hypertension, asthma and migraine headache.

Nervous Tension

These days we often hear of someone suffering from nervous tension or simply nerves. **Dr. D. H. Fink** in his book *Release from Nervous Tension* points out that nervous tensions do not exist exclusively within the nervous system but they reflect the emotional conflicts in the person's mind. Chronic anxieties and frustrations add up to a state of persistant mental stress. The unresolved conflicts act on the autonomic nervous system to bring about the psychosomatic ailments mentioned before. A person under nervous tension displays a marked inability to physically and mentally relax which adds up to the discomfort already induced by the nervous tension.

Chapter 6

Stress-Related Ailments

"The influence of the mind on the body is no transient power. It may exalt sensory functions, or suspend them altogether. It may excite the nervous system or repress it."

Daniel H. Tuke
Nineteenth Century London Physician

We saw how the body-mind works as an integral unit and how stresses originating in the subjective state of the mind as feelings and emotions affect the organic state of the body through the autonomic nervous system and stress hormones. In this section we will discuss some of the more frequently occurring specific bodily ailments which a relaxation seeker must be aware of. A knowledge of the mechanism of their occurrence will help you to adopt the proper physical and mental relaxation exercises, dietary modifications and changes in life style to suit your particular situation.

Body-Mind Partnership

Mind and body constitute an integrated unit. The effect of the mind on the body and that of the body on the mind are described as psychosomatic and somatopsychic respectively. The fact that the mind and emotions influence the well-being of the body has been known to mankind almost in all cultures around the world over the centuries. Recognition of psychosomatic medicine as a speciality branch of the medical science has set the field for unbiased investigations of the role of emotions in the physical health and illnesses.

Doctors **B. F. Miller** and **L. Galton** report that in a recent study of 20 consecutive patients with perforated ulcers, most were due to exposure to extreme situations of stress to which they had reacted with intense anger. Another study using blood pressure monitoring devices revealed that, even in interviews dealing with emotion provoking subjects, particularly anger, there was a marked increase in coronary blood flow, a significant blood pressure rise, and an increase in breathing and heart rate.

Freud demonstrated that the unresolved conflicts at the conscious level of the mind tend to get repressed into the unconscious. There they remain as the hidden source for eventual neurotic or psychotic behavior or a psychosomatic ailment. The connection between guilt feelings and stomach ulcers has now been proven to be an established medical fact.

Psychosomatic Symptoms of Stress

Many people reveal their unhappy mental state through the language of physical symptoms. Some develop allergic type skin rashes; some perspire to excess, particularly in the palms of their hands; some suffer from asthma brought about by mental causes and there are those who complain of frequent urination. Nervous tension in many is shown through headaches. In addition, vomiting, loss of appetite, diarrhea, and heartburn may indicate a person's psychic reaction to an unpleasant stressing situation.

The parts of the body under the control of the autonomic nervous system, such as the digestive track, heart, lungs, urinary bladder, endocrine glands and skin have been known to be particularly vulnerable to the effects of stress. The most common ailments are peptic ulcer, high blood pressure, heart attack, stroke, nervous tension, insomnia, asthma and depression. In addition to these organic disorders, emotional factors and stresses are important factors in producing migraine headaches, mucous colitis, ulcerative colitis, hyperthyroidism and skin allergies.

Stress and High Blood Pressure— "The Silent Killer"

Statistics don't lie. Hypertension or high blood pressure has reached epidemic proportions, particularly in the more advanced industrialized western nations. In the United States of America alone, about 20% of all adults suffer from high blood pressure. It is reported that 40% of all deaths below the age of 65 are due to consequences of high blood pressure. The paradox is that though one out of every five persons has high blood pressure, one-third of them are not even aware of it. However, its ravages on the vital organs of the body such as the heart, brain and kidney are slow and sure, often with fatal consequences.

You may recall that the stressful situations, anxieties and frustrations contribute to the arousal of strong emotions in the mind. **Dr. Herbert Benson** of the Harvard Medical School points out that it is the chronic arousal of the fight or flight response which goes from just transient elevation in blood pressure to permanent high blood pressure.

It is important to remember that the blood pressure is never constant. It keeps changing according to the needs and requirements of the body, and does so frequently in the course of every day. The blood pressure for a normal person at rest can range from 95/65 millimeters of mercury at night to 135/80 in the morning to 150/90 in the evening. The upper value refers to the systolic pressure and the lower value the diastolic. It is normal for many to have slightly increased blood pressure with age, which does not necessarily mean hypertension. A blood pressure value above 160/90 is indicative of high blood pressure.

Atherosclerosis (arterial hardening) is an important factor contributing to high blood pressure. You may recall the role of stress and emotions in this arterial hardening (Chapter 4).

Unlike other organic sicknesses, high blood pressure does not send out any warning signals. It can persist for many years undetected and untreated. Hence, it is often called the "silent killer". Though chronic hypertension begins with no warnings, it could progress rapidly and dramatically, causing damage to the heart, brain, kidneys and eyes. See Figure 7.

Stress and Your Heart

At the very center of healthy and happy living is the heart. No other part of the body is directly pushed into action everytime you experience stress as your heart. Being about the size of a fist and weighing less than a pound, the heart is perhaps the world's most wonderful machine that is built to last a lifetime of continuous action.

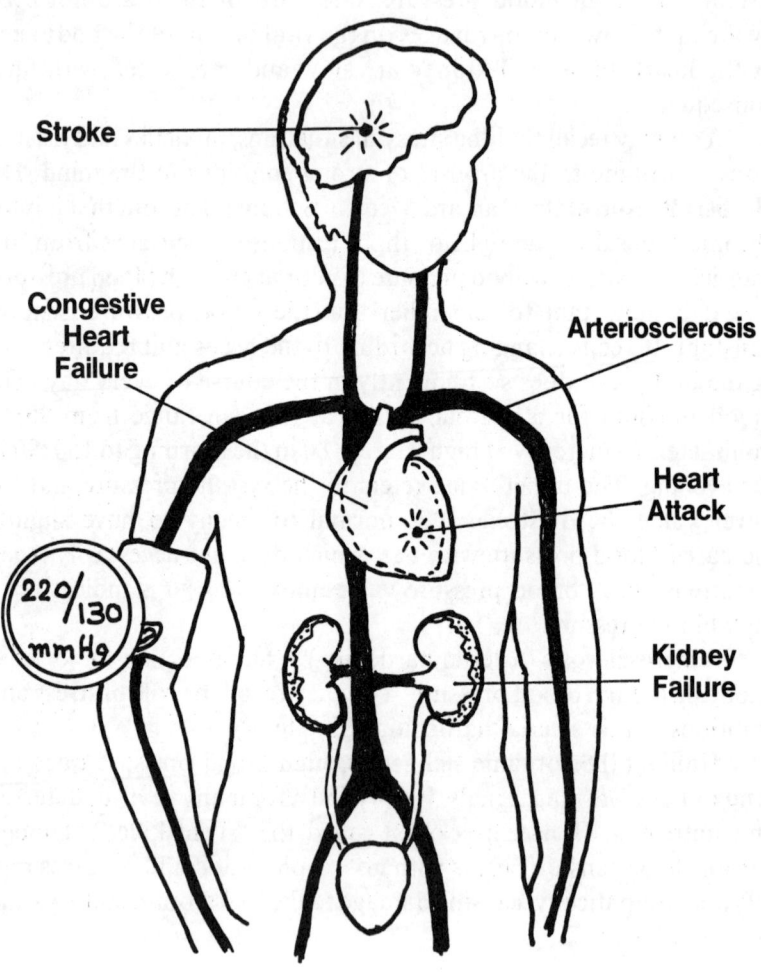

Figure 7. Hypertension damage.

Though small in size, it beats an average of 72 times a minute, 100,000 times a day, nearly 40 million times a year. Every organ of the body is directly dependent on the heart for the vital supply of oxygen and nutrients necessary, which are carried through it by the blood circulation system monitored by the heart.

The heart is a pump and a muscle. It provides the driving force for the circulation of blood through the blood vessels, and it is this fluid pressure commonly referred to as blood pressure. Each thrust of this pump is called a heart beat. Though it normally ranges from 60 and 80 per minute, under conditions of emotional stress and intense muscular exertion the heart beat rate can increase twofold. It must be noted here that a healthy heart is a slow heart. A heart that can take care of the circulation needs of the body with less number of thrusts has more time to relax in between!

Heart Action and Blood Circulation

The heart is literally a coupled double pump, each working independent of the other. The right heart takes care of the pulmonary circulation which serves the lungs where the red cells of the deoxygenated blood eliminate the carbon dioxide and take up oxygen. The oxygenated blood is then carried back to the heart through the pulmonary vein. The left heart pumps the oxygenated blood into the systemic circulation through its arteries to supply oxygen and vital nutrients to all other parts of the body to feed body cells. Figure 8 shows the principal arteries of the human body serving the brain, kidneys and the limbs.

Since the heart is constructed of muscle fibers, the cells of these fibers require oxygen for fuel as all cells of the other parts of the body do. In order to supply its own needs, the heart pumps oxygenated blood to itself through the coronary arteries, while pumping blood to all other parts of the body through the pulmonary and main arteries. See Figure 9. Each heart beat is stimulated by an electrical impulse that originates in a small strip of heart muscle tissue known as the sino-atrial (S-A) node, commonly called a pacemaker.

Angina Pectoris

For whatever reason, if the heart does not receive enough blood to support itself, it is deprived of the oxygen needed for its survival.

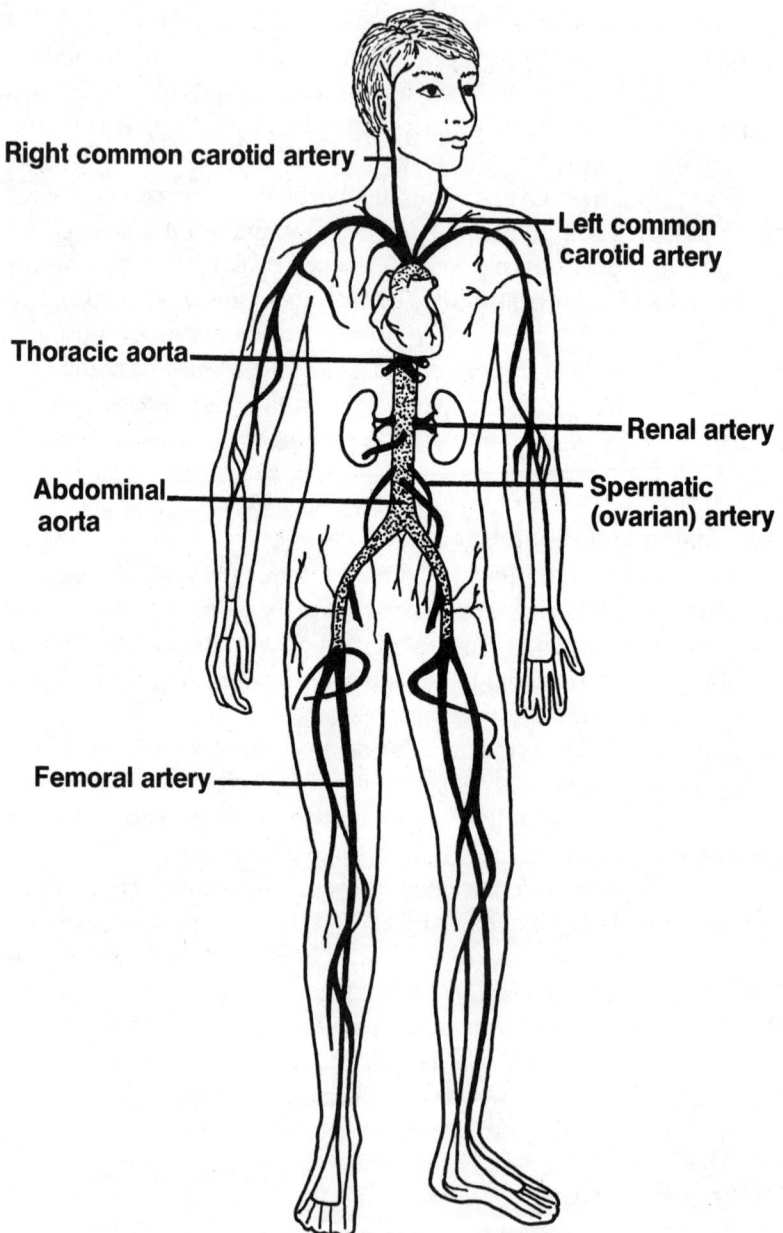

Figure 8. Principal arteries.

Figure 9a. The heart and its arteries.

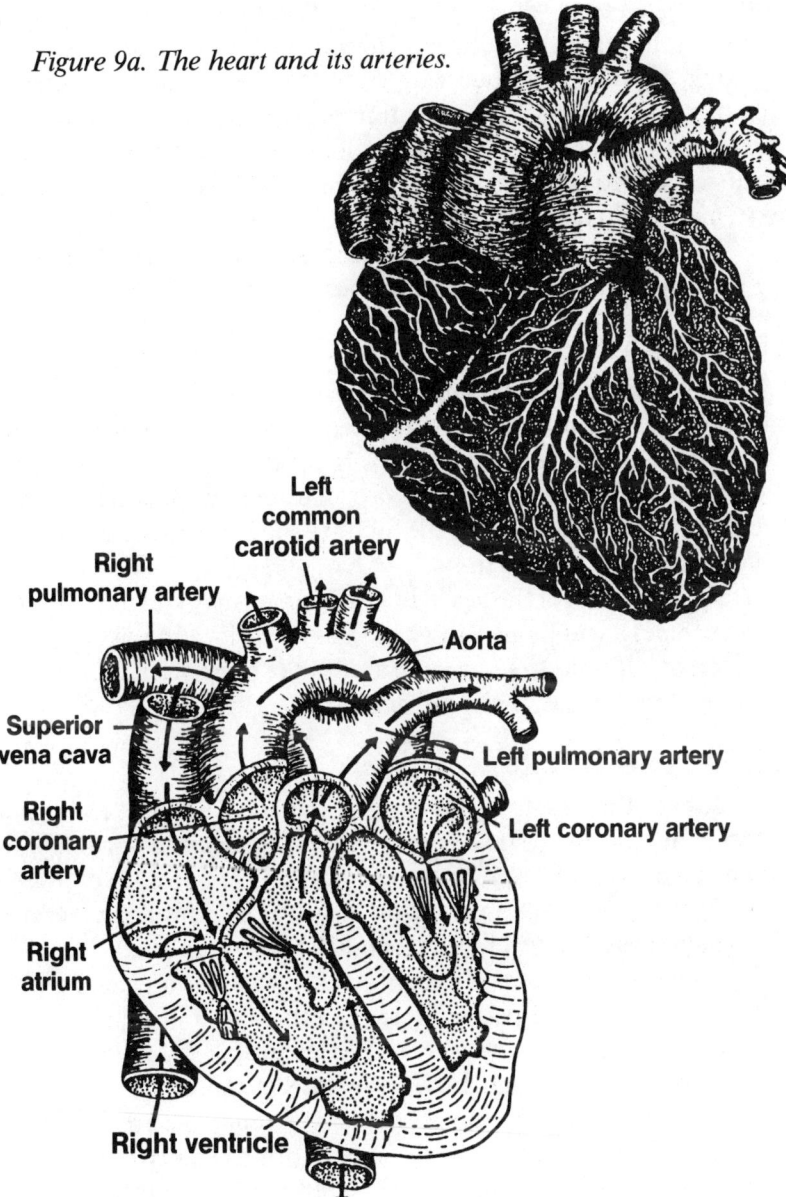

Figure 9b. The Heart and the Main Arteries.

If this oxygen deprivation occurs for a brief time, it results in intense pain over the region of the heart, subjectively expressed as a heaviness, choking, tightness or squeezing over the chest. This is known as angina pectoris. This is an indication of the blockage that is developing in the coronary arteries or a temporary blockage that might have occurred due to coronary artery spasm and platelet clumping under extreme emotional stress.

The physical discomfort due to angina pectoris is usually relieved by rest. No permanent damage has occurred to the heart yet.

Heart Attack

When the blood circulation to the heart is reduced or cut off for more than a few minutes, then that area of the heart which is deprived of oxygenated blood may die. This is commonly known as a heart attack, medically called as a myocardial infarction, which literally means the localized death of the living tissue in the myocardium, the muscular wall of the heart.

If a small part of the heart dies, the person may still live; the dead part becomes a scar tissue. However, if a critical location of the heart is affected or if it occurs over a large area of the heart, then the outcome may be more serious, including death.

Stress and Stroke

Besides the heart, the other vital part of the body that can be affected by emotional stress is your brain. Damage to a portion of the brain can occur as a result of a ruptured artery (Figure 10) or arterial blockage. This is commonly known as a stroke or brain hemorrhage. The brain cells use oxygen at a rate much faster than other cells of the body, and the brain damage occurs quickly when the oxygen supply is interrupted for a brief period more than three or four minutes.

You may wonder how stress is related to stroke. Medical science has recognized that high blood pressure is the culprit. The high pressure under which the blood circulates through the artery can lead to the rupture of the thin walls causing the brain hemorrhage, or it can contribute to the formation of atherosclerosis or the hardening of the carotid artery leading to the brain. It has been mentioned before how emotional stress directly induces high blood pressure, artery spasm

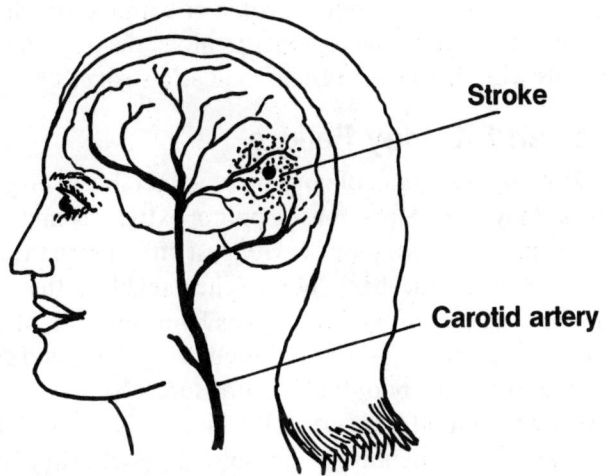

Figure 10. Stroke or brain hemorrhage

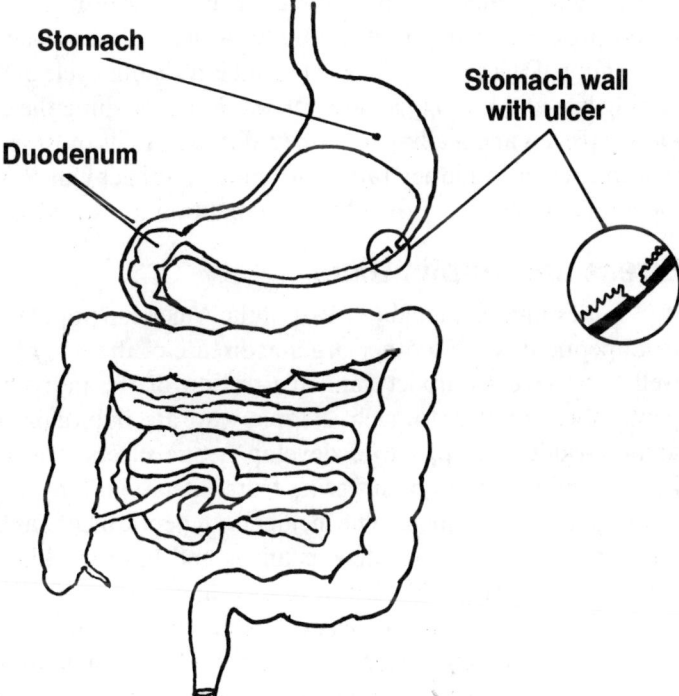

Figure 11. Stomach ulcer.

and platelet clumping. Under chronic or extreme stressful situations these factors can combine together to block the oxygen supply to the brain cells with disastrous results such as a stroke.

Stress and Kidney Failure

Another vital organ of your body vulnerable to emotional stress are the kidneys. The kidneys are a pair of extremely important organs located behind the abdominal cavity, just underneath the rib cage, and on either side of the back bone. They regulate the composition, volume and acidity of the body fluids by means of a filtering system that handles about 15 gallons of blood every hour, and contribute to the regulation of the body's blood pressure.

When the blood pressure in the kidneys is reduced under conditions of arterial hardening of their blood vessels, they secrete a hormone called renin into the blood stream which acts on the minute arteries and capillaries to constrict them. This results in increased blood pressure throughout the body, which, in turn, leads to more hardening of the arteries. The net result is a vicious cycle of the kidney getting less and less oxygenated blood, impoverishing the cells of the kidney tissues and leading to kidney ailments. In its most severe form, this can result in kidney failure when it no longer can eliminate the metabolic wastes from the blood, a condition known as uremia.

Stress and Peptic Ulcer

It is estimated that about 10% of the American population suffers from peptic ulcer. No other organic disease of the body has been so well correlated to anxiety and frustration of the individual as the peptic ulcer of the stomach. People who are habitually tense and anxiety-ridden are prone to develop peptic ulcers. Psychoanalysts have found that persons suffering from intense guilt feelings tend to develop this type of ulcer. The incidence of peptic ulcer has been rated high among busy corporate executives and hard-working surgeons who have not learned the art of relaxation.

Peptic ulcer can be an ulcer of the stomach wall in which case it is referred to as a stomach or gastric ulcer. Or, it can be in the duodenum, the upper part of the digestive tract adjoining the lower end of the stomach. See Figure 11.

How do worry and anxiety start peptic ulcers? As you may know, the inside of the stomach wall is made up of a mucous layer which is glandular and in folds whose surface is pitted with the openings of minute glands. These glands secrete the gastric fluid. The gastric juice contains about 0.5 percent hydrochloric acid, which activates the digestive enzymes and provides the proper acid medium for food digestion.

However, under stressful conditions such as anxiety, worry and frustration, the hypothalamus in the brain activates the autonomic nervous system, which, in turn, activates the glands in the mucous layer. They release a hormone called gastrin which stimulates a group of cells known as "parietal cells" to secrete hydrochloric acid. When the concentration of this acid increases under continuous or frequent stimulation of the glands, hyperacidity of the stomach juices results. When there is no food in the stomach for this acid to work on, it turns on the mucous lining itself. As a result, at some weak spot of the stomach or at the duodenum an ulcer is formed. Chronic hyperacidity worsens the situation.

Stress and Headache

Headache has been known as a universal ailment of mankind. It is mostly a symptom of the stresses and strains of life. But it also can be a warning signal of some serious organic illness. No other bodily pain is so well directly related to the emotional and physiological causes as the headache, and yet it is enigmatic to the sufferer.

The headache pain originates in the nerves that interlace the blood vessels in the brain. Though the brain tissue itself and most of the brain covering are incapable of feeling pain, the nerves of the blood vessels are highly sensitive to changes of pressure within the skull. The pressure changes may be effected by emotional or physical stresses. Of all chronic headaches, tension and migraine headaches account for more than 90 percent. Properly learned and practiced relaxation techniques can easily mitigate them. However, you must consult your physician for persistent headaches.

Tension Headache

This is the most common kind of headache which accounts for an estimated seven of every ten headache occurences. This is also referred to as nervous headache or nervous tension headache. They are usually temporary in nature and disappear under rest and relaxation or mild medication.

The strain in the scalp and neck muscles brought about by sustained physical posture, such as a head position during driving against bright headlights, tends to bring about tension headaches. On the psychological side, when you feel anxious or frustrated, the autonomic nervous system increases the blood pressure in the arteries of the brain, resulting in a tension headache. Current research using electronic equipments that can measure muscle tension accurately has established that the degree of anxiety in a person and the level of his or her muscle tension are directly related.

Migraine Headache

About 5 percent of the American population is affected by migraine headaches. They are much more severe and painful than tension headaches. Intense and throbbing pain is felt in the front and top part of the head, usually on one side only. What causes migraine is still unknown, though many theories have been presented ranging from allergy to glandular disturbances.

Psychologists and psychiatrists have frequently found that migraine is often associated with a personality type, the perfectionist who has fixed attitudes in life and wedded to exact schedules. Many studies have shown that stress is a strong underlying factor, and those who can not adapt themselves with behavior modification are more vulnerable to migraine than others.

It is here that the integral relaxation as presented in this book has its greatest impact. It is not a coincidence that the yoga and meditation practitioners are free from tension and migraine headaches and enjoy the serenity of a healthy and happy life.

Stress and Allergies

Stress has been known for a long time to affect the skin, though it is hard to pinpoint in a cause-and-effect manner. Emotions such as an embarrassment or anger do produce in some persons a rash on the skin of the neck. Chronic worry and anxiety have been known to cause similar rashes and itching. Psoriasis, a skin condition characterized by itchy, red patches that become covered with loose, silvery scales, has been attributed to persistent emotional stress.

Stress and Mucous Colitis

The colon, the lower part of the digestive tract, is subject to inflammation and the condition is known as colitis. A mild inflammation is referred to as mucous colitis or spastic colon. This results from spasms of the muscles in the colon wall which interfere with its normal wavelike motion, thereby inducing cramps and constipation with copious passage of mucous rather than normal feces. Hence, the condition is known as mucous colitis. Emotional stress in the form of nervousness and worry has been a well established cause of the spasms in the colon acting through the autonomic nervous system. This condition can generally be relieved by dealing with the root cause of the emotional tension.

Stress and Ulcerative Colitis

Inflammation and ulcers (open sores) can develop at the end of the colon near the rectum in the large intestine leading to bleeding. This condition is generally known as ulcerative colitis which is a potentially serious ailment. Blood may often be present in the feces and diarrhea may develop. Though medical science has not established an organic cause for the incidence of this serious condition, emotional stress has been recognized as the triggering agent through excessive activity of the thyroid gland.

Stress and Depression

Inability to cope with stress in daily living at the conscious level of the mind slowly leads to a state of chronic anxiety and the defence mechanisms of the mind break down. The person is thrown into a state of feeling dejected or dispirited which is known as a state of depression.

It is quite normal for anyone to hit the blues or go through a brief spell of despondency and grief once in a while. But depression is another matter where a person undergoes a chronic change of mood, marked by sadness, inactivity and self-depreciation. This may be triggered by the loss of a beloved one, loss of a job or money, failure to get a promotion or continous disappointments in life.

When depression occurs, it is not just the mood that is affected. The person may decide that he or she is a complete failure in life, which really is not true. The self-confidence and self-esteem are eroded to the base. Sometimes the person loses all interest in life. The depression may lead to overwhelming fatigue, headaches, sleeping difficulty, appetite loss and digestive upsets. The body's resistance to diseases falls to its lowest ebb. Mental depression is being recognized today as a critical medical problem by many psychiatrists.

Chronic emotional stress alters the chemical balance of the body through the autonomic nervous system, activating the endocrine glands. Depression is attributed to the change in the chemical balance of the body, affecting that of the brain. Depression is beyond the realm of self-help. The person suffering from depression should seek professional help.

Chapter 7

Classification and Sources of Stress

> "Once behavior is set in motion, there is little in human experience that is more disturbing than to be forced to stop what is already underway."
>
> **Franz A. Fredenburgh**
> Author of *Exploring Human Behavior*

Classification provides the basis for an orderly investigation of the phenomena of stress which otherwise may appear too complex or too simple. The word "stress" has now been so generally used that it may encompass situations inducing physical fatigue and pain on one hand and those provoking emotional response on the other. In coping with a stressful situation, it is important to understand the cause and effect of the stressor wherever possible, because the remedial or preventive measures you may take will depend on the nature of the stressor.

Though all stressors result in some form of stress, the nature of emotion induced by a stressor can be very different from each other such as anger, fear, or grief. Accordingly, the associated bodily responses are different; so also are the corresponding brain wave patterns.

Types of Stress

From the manifestation point of view all stresses can be classified into the following seven types:

1. short term physical stress
2. long term physical stress
3. anger provoking stress
4. fear provoking stress
5. grief provoking stress
6. joy provoking stress
7. anxiety provoking stress

Short Term Physical Stress

Short term physical stress is easy to recognize. It occurs when the body's muscles are held in any stressed position too long without relaxing, such as in the case of prolonged sitting or standing in one posture without change. Under these conditions how fatigue is induced in the muscles causing cramps, aches and pain is discussed elsewhere in this chapter.

Long Term Physcial Stress

In the case of long term physical stress, the effects are not immediately manifestive but show up slowly after a long period of time. Typical of them are the effects of stress on the feet. The work load on the feet is astounding when you consider that a 140-pound person brings down on his feet a total work-load of about 200,000 pounds in walking just one mile. The bone structure of the feet with its muscles and ligaments are designed to absorb the impact of body weight and spread it evenly with the least strain. Trouble arises when undue stresses are placed on the feet. It may be due to overweight, poor posture, fatigue or poor fitting shoes. The resulting discomfort may affect other parts of the body as well, such as the spine. Low back problems, joint discomforts and headaches have been known to result from long term stresses on the feet.

Muscle Tension: The Source of Physical Stress

Physical activity is the essence of living, and the body itself is built to move. The muscles of the body are basically responsible for movement. It is the skeletal muscles that cause the body's framework to move, as in walking, running and jumping. They are arranged in pairs of opposite action so that when one muscle contracts, the opposing muscle is relaxed. As an example, you can bend your arm at the elbow and feel the biceps muscle in front contract, and the triceps muscle at the back relax at the same time. See Figure 12.

The skeletal muscles are generally attached to bones by tendons and their gross actions are controlled and directed by the motor area of the cerebral cortex of the brain. They are under your voluntary

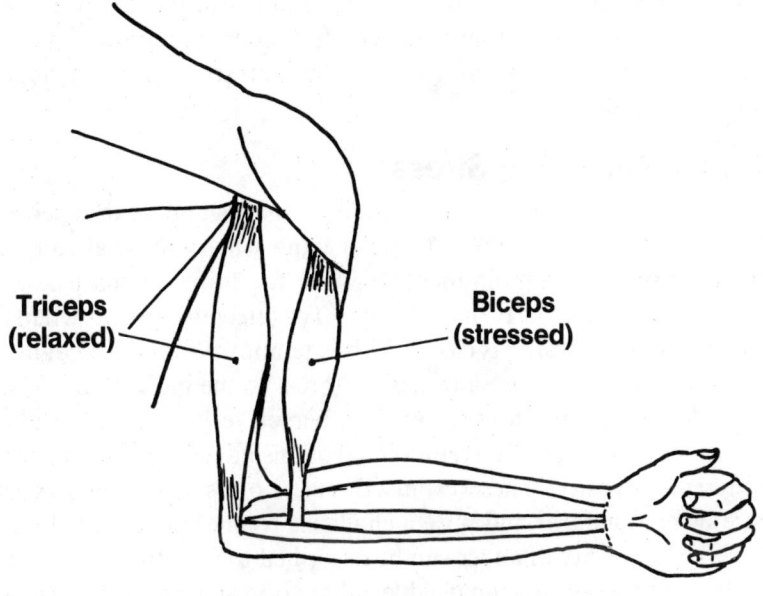

Figure 12. Biceps and triceps muscles.

control, and they are called voluntary muscles. When these muscles contract, the muscle fibers are in tension and they are working. In that process the cells of the muscle tissues use up oxygen and sugar (glycogen) supplied by the blood and gives off carbon dioxide and lactic acid as waste products. If the blood circulation through the muscles is adequate, it brings fresh supplies of sugar and oxygen continuously and the waste products are easily carried away by the tissue fluid draining back into the veins. The waste products are carried in the blood circulation to the lungs, kidneys and skin and excreted.

However, when the contracted or tensed muscle is held without movement over a long period of time in the static position, the tension in the muscle fibers prevents the blood flow through them. This results in the muscles becoming depleted of oxygen and sugar and laden with their own waste products, carbon dioxide and lactic acid, inducing the so-called fatigue of the muscles. Fatigue can cause the muscle to go into cramp-like spasms, causing aches and pains. It is the prolonged tension of the muscles that make you feel more tired at the end of the day than you should be and you may have muscular aches, headache and backache.

Anger Provoking Stress

There is no dearth for stressful situations that provoke anger. For example, when your car won't start at a time when you are already late for an important appointment or when the traffic is snarled, your feelings of annoyance turn into anger. The anger disappears when the car starts or the traffic is eased. This is temporal stress in a cognitive sense and does not pose any serious threat to the individual.

However, situations in which a person feels accused, insulted, contradicted, scolded, misrepresented or misjudged can incite anger of different intensity. These events threaten one's self-image, beliefs, morals or standards and pose a challenge to one's sense of values.

The intensity of anger can be described to vary from uncontrollable fury and rage to manageable indignation and wrath. The arousal of anger is dependent on the personality and mental make-up of the individual. Neuropsychologists consider that the arousal of anger is due to the stimulation of the hypothalamus in the brain, and the intensity of anger is proportional to the degree of stimulation.

The stress factors that bring about the emotional response of anger also set in motion a desire to vent one's feelings and a chain of retaliatory actions may be invoked. Depending upon the circumstances and the personality, the feelings of anger may be suppressed but held in consciousness, repressed (submerged into the unconscious), or expressed by some act of aggression and hostility. Envy and jealousy are subliminal forms of anger towards persons who have something that you desire but could not have or those who had directed their attention from you to somebody else.

Fear Provoking Stress

Our cave dwelling ancesters had to face the constant threat of coming face to face with wild animals and in order to survive, they had to fight or flee from the scene out of fear. Also, they lived in fear of thunder, lightning and other Nature's forces. The modern society has come a long way where many of the fear provoking situations faced by our forefathers are eliminated, only to find them substituted by many "modern" stressors. See Figure 13.

Unemployment, layoff, prolonged ill health and hospitalization are among these modern stressors which incite fear of loss of financial security for many sensitive individuals. Fear of industrial, highway and nuclear accidents loom in the background. Fear of crime on the city streets is another menacing stress for city dwellers. A fluctuating stock market is stress for many stock holders who lose many a night's sleep due to fear of impending losses. Fear of growing old, particularly for some women approaching menopause, has been known to be very stressful.

Grief Provoking Stress

Grief is characterized by a sense of loss, hopelessness and feelings of despair. Typical of the stressful situation that provokes grief is the death of a beloved person. The emotional response is that of an irreplaceable personal loss and a feeling of utter hopelessness. Whereas grief is more intense and usually of shorter duration, the term "sorrow" refers to a deep mental agony caused by a sense of loss and disappointment of long continuing nature. Other personal losses such as loss of a home, business and health could also trigger grief and sorrow.

Joy Provoking Stress

Joy is a basic emotion, and its other forms are happiness, delight and love. Ecstacy refers to a heightened emotional state of joy. These are pleasant emotions and are beneficial for the human wellbeing.

An approaching wedding can not only provoke joy but also some feelings of anxiety. The later is caused due to the needed adjustments in the impending changes in lifestyle that go with marriage. If the anxiety part is predominant, then the wedding could be a real stressor! Postponements and cancellations of many a wedding tell the tale of stress behind the decisions. It is not uncommon to see the contestant of a beauty contest bursting into tears when she is crowned as the beauty queen—out of sheer joy breaking loose from the anxiety!

Commencements, winning in lotteries and arrival of new babies are a few other examples of joy producing stressful events.

Figure 13. stressor in the jungle and office.

Anxiety Provoking Stress

The situations and events that are not so obvious as the ones discussed above are vague, yet stressful, and can be classified as anxiety provoking stress. Whereas fear is a reaction to a specific danger, anxiety is an emotional response that is vague, undefined and objectless, involving a feeling of uncertainty and helplessness. All events and occurrences that constitute a change in routine living of a person, such as change in residence, church, school, job and social activities will lead to some anxiety or feelings of tension.

Sources of Stress

Though it is almost impossible to identify all the sources of stress, the following provides a partial list of some of the major sources affecting most people:
cultural background
society
job
personal finance
physical health
death in the family
changes in lifestyle
retirement
loneliness
interpersonal relationship
personality

Whereas the other factors are self-explanatory, personality is a vague term and needs to be elaborated.

Personality

Each person evolves into a distinct personality of his or her own since birth, and this varying nature is called personality traits by psychologists. The trait denotes a behavior pattern, and it refers to any distinguishable, relatively enduring way in which one person differs from another. Heredity, socio-cultural and religious environments in the development of the child and emotional experiences are considered as major factors in the personality formation. Personality is not fixed, but is developmental in nature with new inputs of learning and new perception of the world around the individual.

Psychologists have tried to classify personality based on traits. The British psychologist, **H. J. Eysenck**, classified all persons into introverts, extroverts, neurotic and psychotic. Although this is too broad a classification to be meaningful, it gives a relative idea of the personalities of people. The majority of normal people are somewhere between a "perfect" introvert and a "perfect" extrovert, whereas the neurotic personality shows up distinctly at the unstable end of the behavior scale. The neurotic personality is described as easily aroused, emotional, moody, touchy, anxious and restless.

Type A Personality

Two American cardiologists, **Dr. R. H. Rosenman** and **Dr. M Friedman** of the Harold Brunn Institute for coronary research at Mt. Zion Hospital in San Francisco discovered a pattern of behavior among a study group of 3500 men who eventually succumbed to heart attack, and they called this "Type A Behavior Pattern". Those less susceptible are called "Type B" personalities.

Type A behavior is characterized by competitiveness, hostility, time urgency, and a high degree of egotism. Being easily aroused and emotional, the Type A person is constantly under stress in daily living and develops high blood pressure as a result.

7 Traits of Personalities

From a stress management point of view, it is more meaningful to recognize the problem-people around us for effective interpersonal relationship. The following seven traits of personalities are easily distinguishable in any company:

1. "Perfectionist" personality
2. "Why Me?" personality
3. "Blamer" personality
4. "Non-truster" personality
5. "Mr. Right" personality
6. "Cynic" personality
7. "Poker-face" personality

"Perfectionist" Personality

The perfect human being is yet to be born. Trying to be a perfectionist in one's undertakings invariably leads to stress. Perfectionists aim to measure their and others' achievements through an undefined scale of perfection and find themselves always falling short. Psychologists consider perfectionist behavior as a subliminal neurosis. The stress management technique to cope with this malady is to try for excellence and not for perfection.

"Why Me?" Personality

At the slightest incidence of something unpleasant the person who wails "why me?" is a candidate for emotional stress leading to grief and possibly depression. The root cause of this behavior is self-pity. Self-pity is an index of immaturity and lack of emotional growth. The attitude of "why me?" prevents the person from developing self-confidence and a balanced view of the world around him or her.

"Blamer" Personality

A person who is quick to blame others or outside events for his own failures all the time can not bring himself to accept his failures and shortcomings. Inability of self-acceptance is one of the major causes of stress in a person. Without self-acceptance, self-improvement and self-excellence techniques do not work. Learning to face one's problems and failures at the conscious level and accepting due responsibility actually strengthens the self-image and reduces the stress.

"Non-truster" Personality

Lack of faith and confidence in oneself is usually revealed as an attitude of distrust towards other people. Such an attitude is a source of perennial stress because meaningful interpersonal relationship is almost impossible for such a person. The business partner who can not trust his companion, the husband or wife who can not trust the other, and the patient who can not trust his doctor are but a few examples of relationships laid on a solid foundation of stress.

"Mr. Right" Personality

The person who asserts always that he is right in his opinions is argumentative and insensitive to the feelings of others. He has no respect for their opinions. This person has a tendency to move against other people in general in the behavioral scale. He is shunned upon and disliked by most of the people whom he lives or works with. This personality trait stems from a deep-seated psychological insecurity. His assertiveness is a subliminal expression and acts as a mask for his subconscious feelings of inferiority. Meaningful interpersonal relationships are not possible for such a person.

"Cynic" Personality

The cynic is one who believes that human conduct is motivated wholly by self-interest and who expects nothing but the worst of human conduct and motives. He completely overlooks the positive potentials of fellow human beings and views the world devoid of moral excellence. Such a person loses the warmth of friendliness towards others and suffers the stress of loneliness though living among people. He or she develops invariably a "sourpuss" personality.

"Poker-face" Personality

The person who hides his true feelings and displays an expressionless face shows little concern for the feelings of others. Such a person tends to develop a double-standard in his code of behavior and is likely to suffer stress in an interpersonal relationship. The poker-face has built a psychological wall around his true self, thereby preventing others from seeing him in the natural color of his mind. The poker-face is in general indicative of extreme selfishness.

PART 3

All About Self-Excellence

Chapter 8

Stumbling Blocks Preventing Self-Excellence

"Before climbing up the ladder, turn around and look at what is holding you down."

Age-Old Proverb of India

If striving for self-excellence is an innate drive in human beings, then what prevents them from attaining that state? There are two aspects to the answer to this question. The first one deals with a set of seven negative factors on the part of the individual which are literal stumbling blocks in the path of self-excellence. You have to rid yourself of these negative factors in your mind before you can attempt to move towards self-excellence. The second aspect deals with a set of seven positive characteristics which are the mainsprings of self-excellence. Together, both the aspects constitute the necessary prerequisites in any action plan towards self-excellence. Let us look at the seven negative factors first:

1. Lack of purpose in life
2. Lack of will and discipline
3. Laziness and procrastination
4. Lack of self-respect and respect for others
5. Lack of patience
6. Emotional turbidity
7. Cognitive distortion

1. Lack of Purpose in Life

Ask the people whom you know reasonably well what their purpose in life is. You will be amazed at the number of people who have not even considered this question. Then compare their way of life and the quality of their living. You will find that those with well defined purposes are more successful and happier in daily living and seem to get more out of life itself than those who drew blank to the question of purpose.

Assigning a purpose introduces meaning to your life, and as a result you will feel new enthusiasm flowing through your veins. Your very thought processes will reorient themselves to align your actions on a course towards the purpose, in the same manner as the scattered iron filings orient themselves to the magnetic field when a magnet is placed before them.

But, you are the one who should set a purpose for your life. It depends on your ideas of living, attitudes, abilities, temperament, and what you seek in your life. The purpose should be of special significance to you, the achievement of which must make your life worth living. It should be appealing to your sentiments, fulfilling to your emotional needs, increase your self-esteem and contribute to a better living. It should not be decided for you by another, however good the intentions might be. You should not try to live the dream of another person.

Goal Setting: Short-term and long-term goals

Once you have defined a purpose in your life, many different elements of your life must be brought into alignment with the purpose for successful implementation, such as interests, needs, and goals of other family members, leisure time, family vacation, etc. Purpose provides you with the direction and control for the flow of your life energy.

Since a purpose is a long-range objective in the far horizon at the time of its conception, you need an action plan to proceed step by step. It is only logical to set short-term and long-term goals for your life-plan in line with your mission of purpose. They can also be viewed from daily, weekly, monthly, quarterly, and annual standpoints to view the progress.

Goals must be meaningful, attainable, and flexible enough to accommodate changes and modifications. Every step towards the goal must be viewed as a stepping stone. Goals must be subjected to periodic review to note your progress. The feedback is essential for further progress and for modifications in the action plan without losing the direction and the purpose.

2. Lack of Will and Discipline—
The dual components of motivation

Will draws the line between success and failure. It is the foundation of all human achievements. It is the lack of will that is the greatest stumbling block in front of your goals. The fate of the new year resolutions is found sealed in the will of the individual. It is the will that makes you move against seemingly insurmountable obstacles.

Lack of will makes decisions and efforts meaningless. Many a person falls into the rut of mediocre living not because of lack of imagination, but because of a lack of will to act. The unfulfilled dreams of success and the unrealized goals stand as everlasting monuments in the life of an individual reminding him or her of his or her good intentions. It is legendary that the path to hell is paved with good intentions. The missing link is the human will.

Of all the creatures on earth only man has the potential in him to invoke an individual will and make his dreams come true. You are the master of your destiny to the extent to which you develop this potential. To a considerable degree you control life's events with a will of your own. Will has the power to overcome hurdles and lead you to your chosen destination. Where there is a will, there is a way.

Determination is the directional tendency rooted in will guiding you in goal-seeking endeavors. Will and determination together form the psychological component of the individual's motivation.

Discipline

Self-discipline on the part of the individual constitutes the physical component of his or her motivation. Will and discipline are the two sides of the same coin; one implies the other. Will is non-manifestive, whereas discipline is manifestive; in simple terms, will shows up through self-discipline. Together they have the potential to take you towards any desired goal—materialistic or non-materialistic, physical or intellectual.

3. Laziness and Procrastination

Nothing in the human nature is more loathsome than laziness. Laziness must not be confused with rest and relaxation, which are beneficial to the body and mind. Being lazy is willfully wasting the precious life energy, which should be harnessed and used for the enrichment of your life. The greatest boon one can ask of is to be alive and healthy, and for this reason the wise consider being alive as a privilege and not a right. How right they are! A privilege should not be abused or misused. Being lazy is downright abuse of your privilege. Besides, laziness prevents your hidden potentials from flourishing since conscious effort during your waking hours is needed to unearth, nourish, and develop them.

Self-fulfillment and creative self-expression are totally not possible for the lazy person. Goal-setting and achieving, however humble the goal may be, is beyond the reach of the lazy. Success and laziness do not go together; oil and water do not mix.

Laziness brings boredom into your life which is the very antithesis of creative living. Boredom breeds indifference to life's natural pleasures and blessings, and drags the lazy person towards sensation seeking. "Kicks," drugs and alcohol are but a few avenues frequented by the sensation seekers, oftentimes leading to a point of no-return.

Procrastination is the tendency to put off things for tomorrow which can be done today. It is partly rooted in laziness and partly in a lack of motivation. The impact of procrastination is unmistakable—poor grades for the student, missed deals for the business man, missed promotions and raises for the office worker, and piled-up household chores for the home-maker. Getting motivated in the event that is being postponed is the key to solving this problem. However, it is up to the individual to reflect on the problem and find a means of motivation. With a positive mental attitude and a coordinated life-plan there will be less room for procrastination when you become serious in managing your time effectively each day.

4. Lack of Self-Respect and Respect for Others

Self-respect implies the confidence in one's worth as a human being and a genuine concern to maintain it. It is the very foundation of a positive self-image. Without it, true happiness and success are not possible for any individual.

Let us first consider the factors that are detrimental to self-respect before discussing the ways and means of improving it. Frequently you hear people saying during the course of a casual conversation:

"I can never do things right"
"I always go wrong"
"I commit too many mistakes"
"I am hanging in there"
"I am not that good-looking"

These statements tell you indirectly how the person views himself or herself. The self-negation is subconsciously permeating the thinking process of the individual, and as a result he or she has such a poor self-image. You can anticipate these people having difficulty in managing their life's problems.

Besides self-negation, a lack of respect and appreciation for one's own achievements, however humble they may be, is a contributary factor to the poor self-image. Esteem and confidence build up by taking pride in your past successes and reflecting on them.

Positive Mental Attitude

In order to build a positive self-image, it is essential that you develop a positive mental attitude. The first and the foremost step is to have faith in you, which means that you are as unique as any other human being on earth, and that you have the potentials for happy and creative living as any body else has. The next step is to think and act positively. Always use positive words in your conversations. Once you consciously project your positive thinking into your words and deeds, the subconscious self-negation slowly recedes, and in its place a positive self-image slowly emerges. Be aware that it takes time and effort, and that it is the only way for you to move towards the development of your potentials for self-excellence.

Respect for Others

Psychologists have recognized it as a basic need of human beings to desire for the acceptance, approval, and recognition from other people. How can you expect the respect of other people, if you don't respect them?

Looking at others as objects to be managed and manipulated is a popular notion in people management. A person nurturing this view may climb up a corporate ladder for a while, but soon will find himself being managed and manipulated by others in the hierarchy often resulting in irrepairable damage to his self-respect. Volumes have been written on the woes of executive stress, which stems primarily from a lack of human sensitivity.

In the family front many heart-breaks could be averted if the spouses showed more respect for the other person's feelings; the interpersonal relationship would not precipitate into an unbearable stress. Being human implies a respect for the other person as a human being, and from it springs a host of healthy attitudes towards self and others.

5. Lack of Patience

In a world of drive-in banks, fast-food restaurants, and instant "kicks," patience as a desirable characteristic seems to have been pushed to the back seat in the individual lives of many people. Yet, it is patience that is needed to wither the stresses of the calamity that might strike anytime in a fast pace of living.

Achievement of all things worthwhile in life requires effort and patience. Patience provides the capacity to endure all that is necessary in attaining a desired goal. It is the most valuable tool for the ambitious aspirant who has set many goals for himself or herself in life. Patience imparts the calm self-possession needed in confronting obstacles and delays and helps to manage stressors effectively.

Patience is the foundation of all other cardinal virtues, such as courage, charity, and tolerance. It is the basic fabric of self-excellence into which are woven all other positive mental attitudes. Positive self-image is a myth without patience.

6. Emotional Turbidity

Emotional turbidity is the state of mind of a person when he flares up with emotional outburst even at a seemingly trivial incident, for example, a parent flaring up at a child for soiling his clothes at play. Oftentimes, the problem is subliminal, that is, the real cause of the emotional expression is at the back of the subconscious without the person being aware of it. The emotion clouds the reasoning, and the person tends to over-react compared to a normal and healthy reaction appropriate to the incident. Chances are that you might have seen this behavior in office where bosses flare up, where peers snap at each other, and at home where the spouse cracks at the least provocative situation.

If you are guilty of this behavior, you need to "look-in" and do some self-analysis to get you out of this disorder. Emotional turbidity is the antithesis of the calmness of mind, and prevents the development of a positive mental attitude towards others. It is the unmistakeable sign of immaturity and a lack of inner growth, intellectually and emotionally. Some psychologists consider this as a distinct neurosis, a behavior disorder. The person displaying emotional turbidity is dubbed as "an infantile adult."

The person suffering from emotional turbidity usually ends up with a poor self-image and low self-esteem, because of his or her tendency to feel remorse and guilty after the emotional outburst. Frequent occurrences of emotional turbidity leaves the person high-strung and nervous. It indicates that he is in a state of prolonged stress, which could make the person chronically and physically tired. Emotional turbidity is a clear symptom of a stressed person, who is yet to go a long way to reach self-excellence—the state at which turbidity does not occur.

7. Cognitive Distortion

We saw before that man is continuously undergoing a process of secondary evolution, which involves his inner development and emotional growth. His perception of the world outside and the environment where he lives plays a great role in the formation of his attitudes and behavior. When his perception itself is lop-sided, faulty, or biased, his very attitudes and value-system in life becomes deviant from those of others, and it is nowhere more apparent than in the areas of money, sex and success. I prefer to call this characteristic as cognitive distortion.

It should be pointed out here that this is quite different from the situation where one feels an internal state of unease when one perceives inconsistencies between one's attitudes or between one's attitudes and his or her own actions. Psychologists call this state as *cognitive dissonance.* In cognitive distortion the person does not experience any conflict within himself, but he clashes head-on with others with different perceptions about the issue involved. It becomes a stressor for him if he is unable to adapt to the challenges of the encounter.

Notions on Money, Sex and Success

Money has occupied the center stage of most people's lives and has taken such a grip on their thinking that it is hard for them to think of an event or action without associating a money value to it. Of course, money is important in the modern world but its due place in the process of living must be delineated by a reasonable and meaningful desire compatible with one's missions and goals in life without sacrificing the humane sensitivity. When a man goes after money as if money is everything to live for, cognitive distortion alienates him from all human values. It becomes a neurosis in itself—an antithesis of self-excellence.

Attitude towards sex has been undergoing continuous transformation and there is no such thing as a standard notion on sex. However, a healthy attitude towards sex is of paramount importance because it involves the feelings of another person and is conditioned by the code of ethics and laws of the society where one lives. Any conflicting attitude has the potential to become a serious stressor.

There is magic in the word "success," particularly in the modern materialistic environment. Consequently, striving for survival is Nature's law while striving for success is man's law. Nature's law is unchanging and immutable, but man's law is subject to change and has limitations. This applies to success seeking as well. The limitations of the individual and the competition in the process become potential stressors to the aspirant. Frustrations and failures are lurking on the road to success. Success implies goal-setting and working towards it. When the goals are not realistic as a result of cognitive distortion, going after them is no different from chasing the mirage—an illusion never to reach.

Chapter 9

Mainsprings of Self-Excellence

"The desire for excellence is also instinctive. While people can live in reasonable happiness without fulfilling this need, life can be much richer and rewarding if you do something well. The degree to which you grow will depend on how much of yourself you bring to the task."

Robert J. McKain
Author of *How to Get to the Top and Stay There*

Self-excellence is a state of inner growth for which there is no yardstick to measure, yet it is realizable by the individual. Since the various factors we discussed before pertaining to the mind remain only at a conceptual level, they should not be construed as clear-cut identities but rather different aspects of the same mind. A considerable degree of overlapping of these aspects is but natural and inevitable in a study of mental faculties and its improvement towards excellence.

In this chapter are presented only the most important characteristics that are considered as the mainsprings of self-excellence and which can be cultivated with intellectual effort for self-improvement. They are:

1. Self-confidence
2. Planned continuous learning
3. Commitment and willingness to work
4. Motivation and enthusiasm
5. Willingness to forego immediate pleasures
6. Emotion management
7. Reaching out to help others

1. Self-Confidence

Your confidence in your own worth as a human being is the foundation for all that life means to you. It leads you to your mental peace and inner happiness, no matter what your materialistic status is. Self-confidence puts you in command of your decisions and actions, and you will not be overly stressed or swayed by the adverse happenings in your life. It is the masterkey for your over-all life management in the family, career, and social environment.

Origin of Self-confidence

Your self-confidence is deeply rooted in the self-image of yourself which is subconsciously formed basically from the inputs of your emotional experiences, rewards and punishments, successes and failures in the past, intellectual realizations, personal value systems, your relative perception of the society you live in, and the constant reactive behavior of those with whom you live and work. The self-image is not a "once-for-all" fixed or unchanging image. Though latently formed in the early years of your life, it is continuously undergoing transformations throughout your life. The emergence of a positive self-image is the source of your self-confidence.

Factors Contributing to Self-confidence

A knowledge of the factors contributing to self-confidence will provide you with the direction of an action plan for behavior modification through intellectual effort. If any of your willful actions or accomplished tasks leaves one or or more of the following impressions in you, it is a positive step towards self-confidence:
1. sense of elation
2. sense of doing right
3. sense of excellence
4. sense of superiority due to power or money (as a result of this action)
5. approval by parents, peers and others
6. health and happiness
7. habit formation

Daily Efforts to Boost Your Self-confidence

Remember that a positive self-image is your greatest asset and that you are solely responsible for it. Only from a positive self-image can spring positive mental attitudes which are essential for success in any of your ventures. You can practice the following techniques in daily living to boost your self-confidence.

1. Use only positive words in your conversations, such as "I can do it."
2. Recall from your memory your past successes and actions that brought you recognition. Re-live, in your mind, the past moments of happiness they brought to you and take pride in them. This will build a "success-frame" in your mind, as **Robert McKain** calls it.
3. Accept your shortcomings and flaws. Without self-acceptance, there will be conflicts in the mind, and the development of self-confidence is not possible.
4. Make the 5-point program presented in Part 4 of this book as a part of your daily activities. It has the potential to bring out the best in you.

2. Planned Continuous Learning

Never before in the history of mankind has there been such a need for the average person to learn for survival and adaptation as that is faced by people in today's world. The invasion of technology into every facet of our living has totally destroyed the simplicity of human living, but as a compensation it has brought in many time and labor-saving devices and creature comforts within easy reach of most people. Also, technology has opened up many different sources of pleasures, means of travel and communications, and techniques for maintaining bodily health.

All these simply mean that a person should learn more and more about the technological innovations to get the most out of them. Also, from a career and professional point of view, continuous learning is a must to keep up with advancements in one's own field of interest, as much as it is from a hobby point of view.

This does not mean to minimize the importance of traditional skill-learning such as painting, weaving, carpentry, etc., as a hobby or trade. Here also, continuous learning is the key to unfold your full creative potentials.

There is another side to learning which lies in its impact on your self-image. Learning contributes to a positive self-image, making you feel good about yourself. In other words, it boosts your self-confidence.

Continuous learning must be tied down to your coordinated life-plan which may have many different goals. Directing your efforts at learning one goal at a time takes you not only closer to that goal, but also brings new meaning to your life. Learning is a voyage of self-discovery. It opens up new avenues and interests in your life which you would not even have thought about before.

Learning is at the core of your intellectual perception of the world where you live. It plays the most important role in your successful adaptation to the stressful challenges encountered in the course of living in a technological world. Self-excellence is wholly dependent on planned continuous learning.

3. Commitment and Willingness to Work

Nothing in the human behavior is more decisive than the action directed by commitment. Commitment is an individual's moral choice which involves him or her in a definite course of action. It binds him or her to the idea or goal either by an intellectual conviction or by an emotional tie meaningful only to the person. Commitment generates the power and momentum to overcome obstacles on the way to reach desired goals.

Self-excellence and commitment go hand in gloves. Each supplements the other. Together, they bring out the best in a person enriching his or her life and, often, enriching the lives of others too.

However, commitment is not an easy-to-come phenomenon. It is an all or nothing event. There is no half-hearted commitment, which simply implies no commitment. It is this factor that draws a distinct line between success and failure in your undertakings. Also, only you can make your commitment. Nobody else can do it for you. Wishes and desires are not commitments, however good-intentioned they may be. You have to make a commitment out of them, if you want their fulfillment. You must either be intellectually convinced of the desire or emotionally drawn to it for the development of a wholehearted commitment.

Commitment means action, and action means work. Willingness to work is the other side of the coin of commitment. The real test of commitment is whether you enjoy doing what you are committed to. A commitment is a source of joy for the person which no amount of money can buy.

This should not be confused with the seemingly busy work of a workaholic, whose behavior stems from a subliminal compulsion or an escapism, lacking the sense and pride of commitment. Instead of a positive mental attitude, the natural sequence of a commitment, the workaholic displays invariably a negative attitude in his undertakings, and he suffers from a sense of insecurity.

Commitment triggers hard work and a sense of discipline to match the committed goal. It is the unmistakable sign of self-excellence.

4. Motivation and Enthusiasm

There is a subtle difference between commitment and motivation. Whereas the former represents a moral choice based on an appeal to your intellect or emotion, the later characterizes a prompting force within you influencing your actions. The motivating force can be a psychological or physiological need, an idea originating at the intellect of your mind, or an intense emotional experience of the past or present. If commitment provides the direction for your actions and goals, motivation serves as the propelling force.

Though the innate instinct for excellence is a powerful motivator for many of his actions at the subconscious level of his mind, man is the only being in the animal world who can consciously induce in himself motivations and, thereby, pursue a life of excellence. Motivation may have its origin in intellectual stimulation and curiosity about the phenomenal world, or it may arise from the desire to achieve in the competitive world.

While motivation is the force behind human endeavors, enthusiasm is the feeling of excitement in the action or involvement. Enthusiasm has a synergistic effect in motivated endeavors. It not only boosts your commitment, but also makes hard work lighter.

Fortunately, enthusiasm is a cultivable characteristic, and it is in the power of the individual to consciously develop the habit of throwing in enthusiasm in one's undertakings, however insignificant it may seem. Habitual enthusiasm builds up a positive mental attitude—the basic ingredient in your strong self-image.

Also, enthusiasm is contagious in interpersonal relationships—in home, office or elsewhere. It builds up the cooperation of others in joint ventures and is a mark of leadership. Enthusiasm is the lingering fragrance of self-excellence.

5. Willingness to Forego Immediate Pleasures

All worthy goals need planning, and worthy achievements need effort. All successes call for a certain amount of sacrifice. The willingness to forego immediate pleasures for the sake of long-term benefits is not only a sign of maturity of a person, but also a requirement for a goal-oriented living.

Long-term goals, particularly, need coordinated planning of your life style to accommodate additional effort needed on your part, both for planned continuous learning and for actions towards the goal. Often this means a sacrifice of your personal time which you might, otherwise, have spent watching television or playing tennis. This does not mean "all work and no play" for the goal seeker. It only emphasizes the need for an effective utilization of your available time and energy to move towards your goals and to rearrange your priorities in your time management.

Goals, of course, when achieved bring you lasting happiness. Besides, the pleasant awareness that you were moving towards your goal by virtue of your planning and effort compensates adequately for your sacrifice elsewhere.

Buying a dream house, going on a long vacation to an enchanted place, paying for children's future college education, working toward professional advancement, trying to maintain physical fitness, etc., are all worthy long-term goals whose benefits transcend the sacrifice of immediate pleasures. These goals, in themselves, have the potential for preventive stress management and pave the way for an enriched life.

No matter what kind of planned life you try to lead, certain small pleasures need not be sacrificed at all—such as enjoying a cup of coffee in the quiet corner of a restaurant, looking at the beauty of the flowers in the garden, and watching the rolling clouds in the far horizon. The time they take may be small, but the rewards they give are bountiful. They provide genuine relaxation to the body and mind. Admiring Nature is to become one with Nature, when the stressors of the man-made world disappear.

6. Emotion Management

To become emotional is human. It is the very spice of living. Yet, emotions must be handled with care. Anger, fear and grief are the negative emotions which have the potential to ruin the life of any person, if he or she succumbs to them. Even the positive emotion of joy needs to be kept within bounds. When emotion takes over the mind, the intellect and its power of reasoning are pushed overboard, with the result that the person's decisions and actions no longer reflect his best interest in the long run.

Spontaneous display of anger is detrimental to your mental health. It can ruin friendships and interpersonal relationships. But, learning to manage anger is a step towards self-excellence. Such a learning calls for a self-analysis as to why you get angry in the first place. Though the arousal of anger is a complex psycho-neurological phenomenon not fully understood yet, psychologists have traced it to the "value-system" or "sense of values" of the person.

When an event in the phenomenal world is viewed by the person as a threat to his survival or as a conflict to his subjective sense of values and expectations, the emotion of anger is triggered. Anger management calls for a few extra moments of deliberate reflection on the event, rather than a spontaneous explosion of word or deed. The few moments of secondary thinking will help in broadening the perspective of the event, and also provide an opportunity for a calculated alternate course of response to the event.

There is nothing wrong in a verbal expression of anger so long as it does not trigger a conflict in the value-system of the other person. How you say it is as important as what you say. But, the key is in your immediate return to a state of composure and equanimity.

Anger management is possible only when you develop a healthy sense of respect for the other person as a human being who has as much right for his subjective sense of values as you have for yours. Anger creates more problems than it can solve. For this reason the wise consider that to be able to control and transcend anger in life is the greatest of all virtues.

7. Reaching Out to Help Others

All people are equal in the eyes of law. But, unfortunately, all are not equally placed in the society, and worse yet, all are not equally born physiologically and psychologically. All are not equally young and strong, and all are not healthy and wealthy equally either. It is a fact of life that there are many people in our societies who can not fully take care of all their needs themselves—the physically and mentally handicapped, the elderly, the sick, the poor, the children of broken homes, the victims of crime and war, and the genuinely unemployed.

It is cruel to say that these people have as much opportunities as anybody else has in a free society like ours because life has not been kind to all people alike. Besides, who knows, you may be the one who needs help at some point of your life, if not right now. As much as you are trying to develop and live to your full potential, it is your duty to help those who need help to develop their uniqueness and potential for a creative living.

Noble as it is, altruism, the consideration for others' needs, is also instinctive in all bioorganisms, including man. It is a weapon for collective survival, and as such everyone has a stake in it. Besides, there is genuine happiness in the act of giving and sharing. The pleasant feeling that you are helping someone less fortunate than you are is enough to kindle the sense of self-esteem in you.

Reaching out to help others is a sign of self-excellence. No special resources, nor lots of money, nor power are required to be altruistic. A genuine desire to help others in whatever form within one's means is all that is needed. Reaching out has a therapeutic value in stress management. It can make you feel good about yourself and strengthen your positive self-image.

PART 4

5 Steps To Self-Excellence

Chapter **10**

Step 1—Towards Bodily Excellence Through the Pulsative 20 Minutes

"Faithful practice of Hatha Yoga can bring relief from tension, improve circulation and complexion, and relieve chronic fatigue. It will also help develop poise, balance, flexibility, abundant energy and vitality, a trim and firm figure, and the ability to relax."

Kathleen I. Hitchcock
Author of *Hatha Yoga*

Step 1 aims at physical excellence so that your body can look and feel at its best, slim and trim with vibrant health. You should check with your doctor before taking this step if you have any health or heart problems. If you are overweight or underweight, you should first concentrate on bringing your body weight to that recommended by your doctor. Step 1 is primarily concerned with physical exercises and relaxation techniques with emphasis on a healthy heart. Coronary excellence is the basis for physical excellence. Step 1 is called "the pulsative 20 minutes" to indicate the minimum duration needed for active physical exercise of your choice. Attainment of physical excellence reflects the homeostasis of the body, the desirable state of good health.

50% Elevated Cardiopulmonary (ECP) Balance

For physical excellence you should exercise to the point where the heart beat increases by 50% of its normal rate. Assuming that an average normal heart beat rate per minute as 72, a 50% increase over this rate is 108 beats per minute. Doing the exercise at a level not more than 108 beats per minute for a minimum period of 20 minutes is considered as the maintenance level for adequate cardiovascular endurance. This is referred to as the state of 50% elevated cardiopulmonary (ECP) balance. Using a stopwatch or a wristwatch, it is easy to check the heartbeat rate by counting the pulse rate at your wrist for one minute during your exercise program. See Figure 14.

Active Exercises for Health and Relaxation

Many people can not understand that active physical exercises can bring relaxation to the tensed muscles and provide relief from fatigue. However, when you realize that muscles relax only through movement which improves the blood circulation through their fibers, it will not be a surprise. Muscles use up oxygen and glycogen (sugar) and give off carbon dioxide and lactic acid as waste products. It is the blood circulation through the muscles that ensures the supply of the former and removal of the latter. When the muscles become depleted of oxygen and glycogen and loaded with their own waste products, they become stiff and sore. As a result, aches and pains develop in the muscles.

Active physical exercises provide the opportunity for movement in the muscles when the blood supply increases due to the speeding up of the circulatory and respiratory system. The muscles are freed from the residual tension and become relaxed.

The active exercises, most suited for physical excellence, muscular relaxation, and release from stress, can be grouped into four basic categories. They are:
1. conditioning exercises
2. aerobic exercises
3. Hatha Yoga
4. relaxation games and sports.

Conditioning Exercises

Janet Wessel and **Christine Macintyre,** in their book *Body Contouring and Conditioning through Movement,* point out that movement is a potent force in helping you to resist the ill effects of physiological and psychological stresses and to release undue tensions. Movement improves the strength, flexibility, and endurance of the

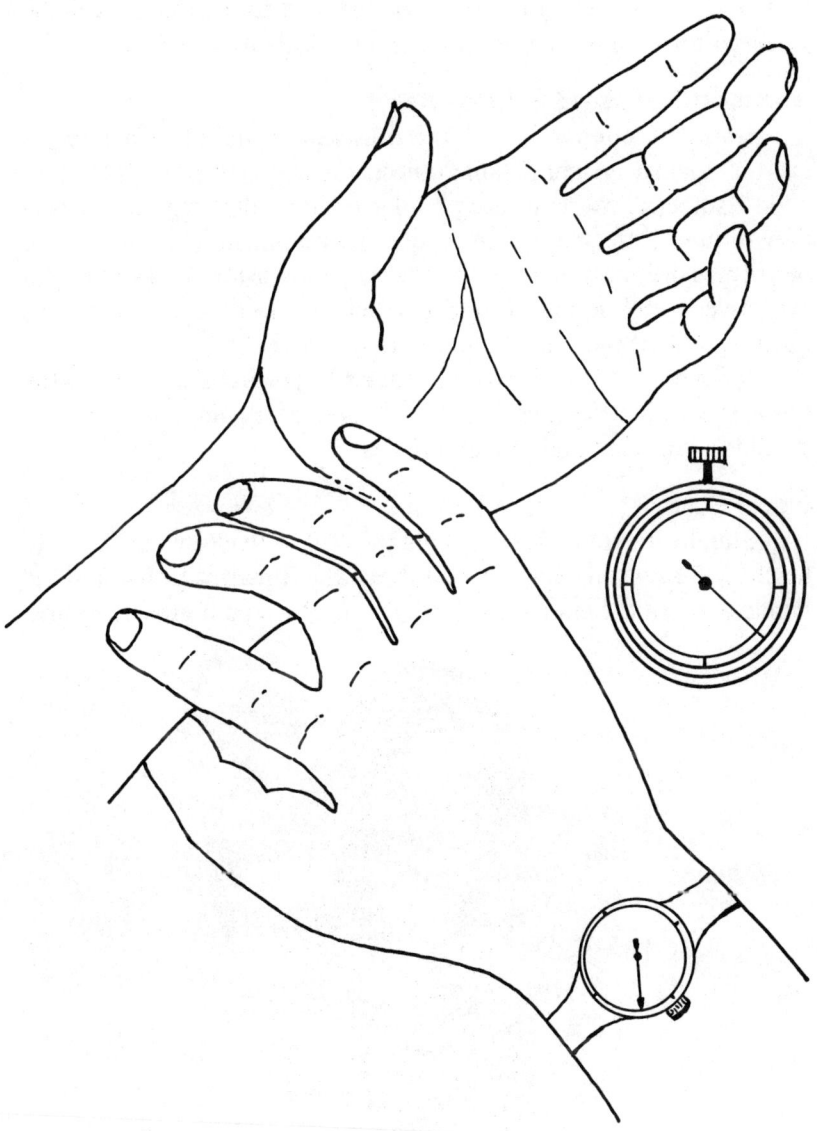

Figure 14. Ckecking the pulse rate.

muscles and induces relaxation in them. This condition can be achieved through isometric, isotonic, or calisthenic exercises.

Isometric Exercises for Stress Relief

Isometric contraction of the muscles occurs when a force is exerted against an immovable object, such as a wall or one's own hand. Isometric exercises are popular for the following reasons: (1) they require little space and no special equipment; (2) they can be performed in a short time; (3) they develop muscle tone and strength in a relatively brief period of time; (4) they help to relax a sore muscle quickly, and (5) they can be built into daily life

In his book *Physical Fitness,* **Robert V. Hockey** recommends the following isometric exercises to be used every day to relax the shoulder, arm, and abdominal muscles.

Elbow Push

Stand with your back touching the wall, with elbows at shoulder height and also touching the wall. Keep the forearms flexed and the hands beneath the chin with palms down. Press your elbows against

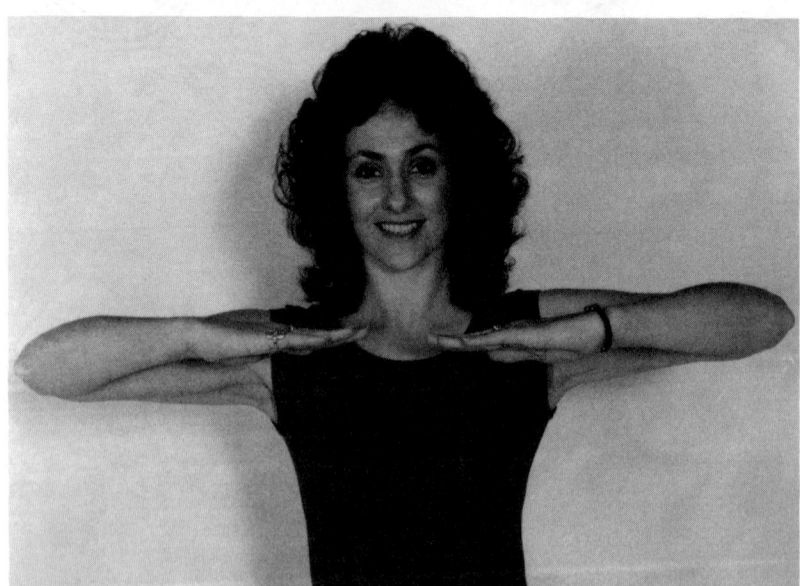

Figure 15. Elbow push.

the wall. Hold the contraction for 5 seconds. Release and repeat 5 times, paying attention to proper breathing. See Figure 15.

Hand Push

Stand with your palms together and the elbows raised to shoulder height. Press the palms together as hard as possible. Hold the contraction for 5 seconds. Release and repeat 5 times. See Figure 16.

V-Sit

Sit on the floor, place the hands on your hip, and lean backward until the trunk forms an angle of approximately 45 degrees with the floor. Keeping the legs straight, raise the feet approximately 12 to 20 inches from the floor forming a V position. Hold the contraction for 5 seconds. Release and repeat 5 times. See Figure 17.

Isotonic Exercises

Isotonic contraction occurs when the muscle contracts and shortens, and at the same time movement takes place. Most common exercises, such as calisthenics and weight lifting, involve isotonic contractions.

Figure 16. Hand push.

Isotonic exercises make use of light equipment such as barbells, dumb-bells, iron boots, or ankle weights. These exercises are primarily meant for building muscle strength, tone, and endurance rather than for relaxation or stress relief. However, if you have access to them, and you enjoy using them, there is no reason why you should not use isotonic exercises for stress relief at the end of a day's sedentary work.

Calisthenics for Stress Relief

Ideal exercises for relaxation and stress relief are simple calisthenics and aerobic exercises. The President's Council on Physical Fitness has developed an adult physical fitness program, consisting of a progressive series of calisthenics combined with exercises designed to develop cardiovascular endurance. This is a graduated fitness program for adults to proceed from level 1 to level 5 progressively, as your physical fitness level improves. The first three levels are well suited for relieving physiological muscle tension which can be used every day. The type of exercises and the minimum number of repetitions involved for women and men are presented in Table 1.

Figure 17. V-sit.

Adult physical fitness program for women—first three levels

Exercise	Level I	Level II	Level III
1. Toe touch	5	10	20
2. Sprinter	8	12	16
3. Sitting stretch	10	15	15
4. Knee push-up	8	12	20
5. Sit-up	5	10	15
6. Leg raise	5 each leg	10 each leg	16 each leg
7. Flutter kick	20	30	40
8. Circulatory activity (choose one for each workout)			
Walking/jogging	½ mile (120 steps /min.)	½ mile (jog 50 yd; walk 50 yd.)	¾ mile (jog 50 yd.; walk 50 yd.)
Rope skipping	2 series (skip 30 sec.; rest 60 sec.)	3 series (skip 30 sec.; rest 60 sec.)	3 series (skip 45 sec.; rest 30 sec.)
Running-in-place	2 min.	3 min.	4 min.

Adult physical fitness program for men—first three levels

Exercise	Level I	Level II	Level III
1. Toe touch	10	20	30
2. Sprinter	12	16	20
3. Sitting stretch	12	18	24
4. Push-up	4	10	20
5. Sit-up	5	20	30
6. Leg raise	12 each leg	16 each leg	20 each leg
7. Flutter kick	30	40	50
8. Circulatory activity (choose one for each workout)			
Walking/jogging	1 mile (120 steps /min.)	1 mile (jog 100 yd; walk 100 yd.)	1½ miles (jog 200 yd.; walk 100 yd.)
Rope skipping	3 series (skip 30 sec.; rest 30 sec.)	3 series (skip 1 min.; rest 1 min.)	5 series (skip 1 min.; rest 1 min.)
Running-in-place	2 min.	3 min.	4 min.

Table 1. Adult physical fitness program.

Toe Touch

Stand at attention with legs straight and feet together. Bend the trunk forward, touch the fingers to the ankles, to the top of the feet, to the toes, and return to the starting position. This is counted as one repetition. See Figure 18.

Sprinter

Squat with hands on the floor with fingers pointing forward. Extend your left leg to the rear. With a bouncing movement, reverse the position of the feet by bringing the left foot level with the hands and extending the right foot backward. By bouncing, reverse the feet again, returning to the starting position. This is counted as one repetition. See Figure 19.

Figure 18. Toe touch.

Sitting Stretch

Assume a sitting position on the floor with legs spread apart and hands on the knees. Bend forward at the waist, extending the arms as far forward as possible and then return to the starting position. Count this as one repetition. See Figure 20.

Figure 19. Sprinter.

Figure 20. Sitting stretch.

Straight-leg Sit-up

Assume a sitting position on the floor with legs stretched in front. Interlock your fingers behind the neck with gentle pressure on it. With hands in this locked position, bend forward lifting the right elbow as far as possible. Return to the original position and bend forward, lifting this time the left elbow as before. Return to original position. This is counted as one repetition. See Figure 21.

Leg Raise

Lie on right side on the floor with right arm fully extended above the head. Rest your head on it. Lift the left leg approximately 24 inches off the floor, keep it straight, and then lower it. Count this as one repetition. When the desired number of repetitions are completed on one side, reverse the position and repeat the exercise. See Figure 22.

Flutter Kick

Lie face down with hands tucked under thighs. Arch your back by lifting the chest and head off the floor. Then kick your legs, moving 8 to 10 inches apart, using the hip as the anchor. Count each kick as one repetition. See Figure 23.

Figure 21. Straight-leg sit-up.

Figure 22. Leg raise.

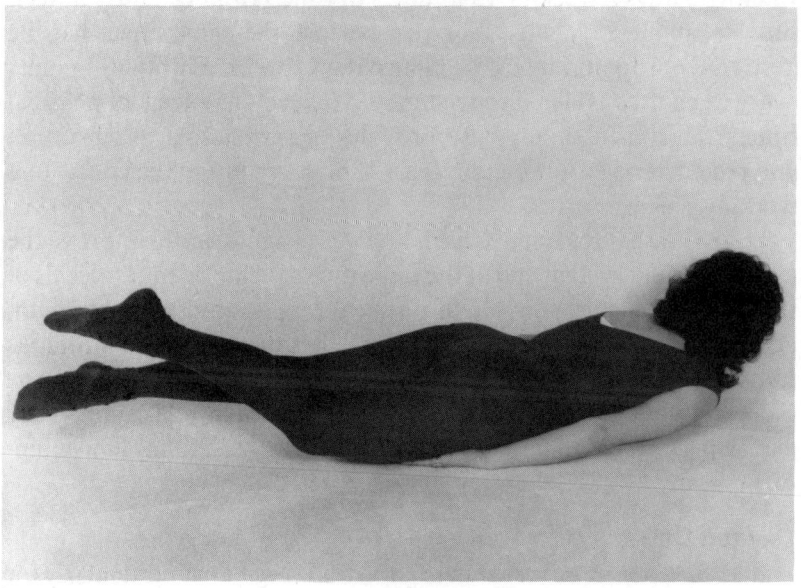

Figure 23. Flutter kick.

Aerobic Exercises for Stress Relief

Aerobic exercises are well suited for physiological relaxation. Aerobics differ from recreation, isometrics, and isotonics in that you pick an activity and gradually—over a period of several weeks—build your body up to demanding large amounts of oxygen for the sustained length of time. Aerobic exercises are those that usually can be maintained for at least 10 minutes and during the performance of which no true oxygen debt is incurred.

Based on four years of extensive investigation and research in which 15,000 United States Air Force personnel participated, **Dr. Kenneth Cooper** developed a point system to rate various common everyday activities such as walking, jogging, running, rope skipping, stair climbing, swimming and cycling. The unique feature of this system is that it allows an individual to equate different activities in terms of energy expenditure and, in this way, to determine which kinds of activities are best suited for her or him and also how long one must participate in an activity to attain beneficial results.

For example, for an average 35 year old person, 30 minutes of walking 5 days a week or 15 minutes of rope skipping 5 days a week provide about 22 points. For this person, the same effect can be derived from 16 minutes of running 5 days a week. Earning 24 points every week is considered the maintenance level for excellent physical fitness. This, incidentally, also provides the physiological relaxation and relief from neuromuscular tension built up during the course of a working day.

Aerobic exercises have been known to significantly improve the cardiovascular system and at the same time develop adequate levels of the other three components of physical fitness—muscular strength, endurance, and flexibility. Therefore, because of the continuous movement and flexing of body muscles, aerobic exercises have the highest potential for physiological stress relief and relaxation. They can be performed outdoor or indoor, and they need minimum equipment, if any.

Oxygen Debt

In fact, aerobic exercises are good for every body, particularly for those with a sedentary type of living. During aerobic, your whole body moves, heart beats faster, breathing becomes deeper, blood vessels expand to carry blood and oxygen to the working muscles, and you start to sweat. Your lungs expand and take in more air, which means more oxygen. Thus, your body adapts to the rigors of the physiological movement without falling into oxygen debt, resulting in the release of muscular tension, and providing relaxation to the very same muscles.

Caution

However, a mention of caution must be made here for the neophyte. Start an aerobic program only after consulting your physician, and then proceed slowly to reach the maintenance level in 10 to 12 weeks in the exercise of your choice.

It will be worthwhile for you to study the pros and cons of the various aerobic programs and choose the one you like best which you can build into your daily life. No matter what exercise program you choose, discipline yourself to practice it regularly, at least 5 times a week, a minimum of 30 minutes each session. My recommendation always is to combine aerobics of your choice with some calisthenics to flex the system of muscles of your body overworked in your particular daily routines.

Rope Jumping—The Perfect Exercise

Of all the aerobic exercises, acclaimed as the perfect exercise to suit most people of both sex is the simple rope jumping, also popularly known as skipping. Unlike stationary running, it involves enough forward movement to take the impact off a purely vertical plane. As a result, the danger of foot, leg and ankle pain is lessened. Also, in rope jumping the muscles of your arms, shoulders and upper body get more workout than in running in place, thus providing more toning action. See Figure 24.

This exercise is inexpensive; all you need is a simple rope. It can be done indoors or out, and so you don't have to blame the weather for being unfavorable. **Greg Campbell**, in his book *Joy of Jumping,* points out that jumping rope is the best all-around exercise you can find. Research data indicate that rope jumping promotes cardiovascular endurance, thereby improving overall physical fitness.

Curtis Mitchel, the author of *The Perfect Exercise,* believes that jumping a rope, simple and easy as it were, produces an astonishing reaction in the body and mind, reducing the neuromuscular tension and fatigue.

Starting with 50 jumps the first week, progressively add 10 skips each day. In six weeks you should be able to do 500 skips continuously, and keep that as the maintenance level. Keep your practice at a regularity of at least 5 days a week. Even if you can not do 500 skips continuously as you set out to accomplish, keep doing a total of 500 skips each session as a fitness level for muscle relaxation.

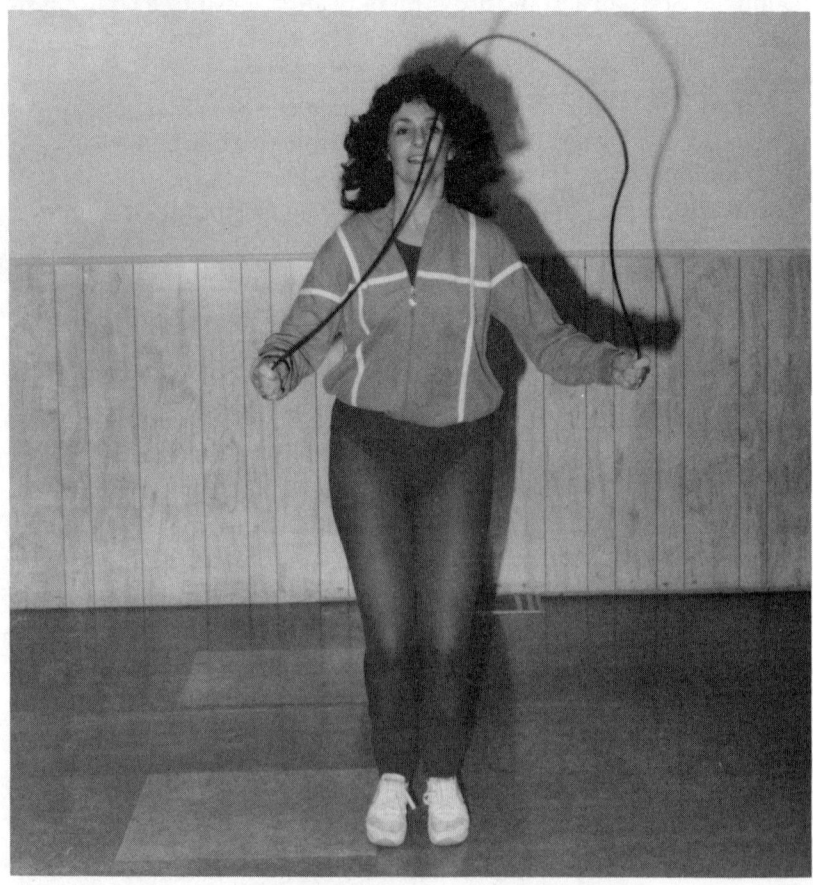

Figure 24. Rope jumping.

Hatha Yoga—
The Natural Physiological Toner and Relaxer

Hatha Yoga is that branch of the Yoga philosophy which deals with control and purification of the physical body, keeping it fit for the concentration of the mind. It specifies many *asanas* or physical postures which are primarily intended to harmonize the body and mind to achieve concentration.

The discipline of the body is as much necessary for the attainment of concentration as that of the mind. Yoga lays down many rules for maintaining the health of the body and perfecting the asanas. The asanas, in turn, become the stepping stones for the higher goal of the aspirant, namely, to reach a state of superconsciousness. The process of perfecting the asanas has come to be known as Yogic exercises or simply as Yoga in the West.

Obviously, the health benefits of the Yogic exercises are incidental. However, the therapeutic and relaxation effects of these exercises have drawn the attention of physical culturists everywhere and have established a legitimate place among the modern physical culture and fitness systems.

The basic difference between Yogic exercises and general physical exercises lies in the manner in which muscle movements are effected. Whereas fast, even violent, movements are carried out in other exercises, Yoga emphasizes slow and gradual movements with proper breathing and relaxation, combined with a passive but concentrated mental state. Thus, these exercises hold the key to provide some control over the autonomic nervous system, which has normally been considered to be beyond voluntary control.

In her book *Hatha Yoga,* **Kathleen Hitchcock** affirms the proven fact that faithful practice of Hatha Yoga brings relief from muscular tension, improves blood circulation and complexion, and relieves chronic fatigue. This practice helps to develop poise, balance, flexibility, abundant energy and vitality, and above all a trim and firm figure. In addition, Yoga exercises build slowly and steadily an ability to relax at will. It is this fact that has found Yoga a permanent place in all stress management programs. Many serious students of Hatha Yoga have testified that their very outlook towards life has changed, making them relaxed and self-assured individuals.

106　　　　　　　　　SELF-EXCELLENCE

Figure 25-1.

Figure 25-2.

Yoga sun worship postures.

Figure 25-3.

Figure 25.4.

Figure 25.5.

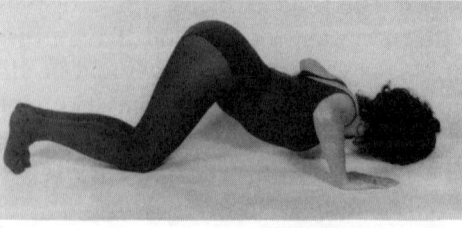

Figure 25.6.

Figure 25-7.

Figure 25-8.

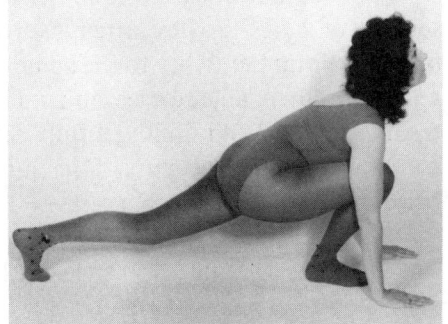

Figure 25-9.

Figure 25-10.

Figure 25-11.

Figure 25-12.

Figure 25. Yoga sun worship postures. Positions 1-12.

Yoga Sun Worship Postures

The classical 12 positions of the Sun Worship Yoga exercise are shown in Figure 25. They are practiced early in the morning facing the sun. The 12 positions are done consecutively, each leading naturally into the next. The complete routine takes about 5 minutes to complete; each separate position is held for 5 seconds. The sequential movements, executed slowly and gracefully, involves 5 breathing cycles of inhalation, holding, and exhalation.

Carried out daily either in the morning or as a starter before a session of Yoga or any other exercise program, this series of 12 postures bring flexibility to the spine and every joint in the body, flex and strengthen all muscles and increase breathing capacity. As a result, the body and mind get fully relaxed.

Step by step procedure of the Sun Worship Yoga exercise is given below.

1. Facing the sun or the east direction, stand upright with legs together and knees straight. Hold your hands in front of you, in prayer-like fashion.
2. Inhaling through the nose, separate both hands, stretch the arms above your head, and simultaneously bend backward. Hold for 5 seconds.
3. Exhaling through the nose, now bend forward and place your hands flat on the floor by the side of feet or hold the ankles. Touch your forehead to the knees. Hold for 5 seconds.
4. Inhaling through the nose, slowly slide right leg straight back. Bend left knee, keeping hands and left foot firmly planted on floor, and stretch head and neck upward. Hold for 5 seconds.
5. Hold your breath and extend left leg straight back along side of the right leg, keeping arms straight. Hold for 5 seconds.
6. Exhaling through the nose, bend your knees to the floor, and then lower chest and forehead to touch the floor. Hold for 5 seconds.
7. Inhaling through the nose, lower your entire body to the floor, keeping toes flat. Place hands flat on floor firmly in front of the chest, arch back, and throw your head backward, bending the spine to the maximum. Hold for 5 seconds.

8. Exhale and lift the body. Keep the feet and heels flat on the floor until your body forms a triangle position. Hold for 5 seconds.
9. Inhale and slide your right foot forward, bending the knee, to the level of the hands. Look up. Stretch neck and head upward. Hold for 5 seconds.
10. Exhale and bring the left leg forward. Keep the knees straight and bring forehead down to the knees. Hold for 5 seconds.
11. Inhaling through the nose, raise your body slowly into upright standing position, and stretch your arms above the head and bend backward. Hold for 5 seconds.
12. Exhale through the nose and straighten your spine. Slowly lower the arms to sides and relax completely.

Other Yoga Exercises

Hatha Yoga ia an art and science by itself. Countless postures have been postulated. Yet, it is an experimental science, allowing room for innovative postures to the practitioner for his needs and outlook. From very simple to very complicated postures are prescribed in the literature. Depending on your interest, you can further explore them for your best advantage in seeking relaxation and physical fitness. Fortunately, many good books on Yoga are available in most public libraries.

Relaxation Sports

Consult with your physician to choose the right type of sports, if you are a sport-minded person, to suit your health conditions. Sports can be relaxing and also can contribute to your overall physical well-being. Highly competitive and rigorous sports must be avoided, since they may constitute a source of stress instead of providing relaxation. Activities like swimming, golf, tennis, handball, canoeing, badminton, hiking, squash, horseback riding, skating, cycling, bowling, and rowing can be physically stimulating and mentally relaxing. See Figure 26.

No matter what sport you indulge in, you will derive the most benefit from it only when you enjoy doing it and build it into your living pattern with a certain frequent regularity, at least 3 times a week or every alternate day. Such a regularity will pave the way for body conditioning and relief from residual muscle tension accumulated during the intervals.

Cardiovascular Excellence and Stress Test

Different exercise tests, such as the treadmill, bicycle, steps, etc., are used to clinically evaluate the cardiovascular condition of the person through electrocardiogram (ECG) recordings. Check with your doctor for an evaluation of the condition of your heart before you get started on any vigorous exercise program. In Figure 27 is seen cardiologist **Dr. Ravindranath Bhirud** administering the treadmill stress test to the author in the Montgomery General Hospital.

Figure 26. Relaxation sport: tennis.

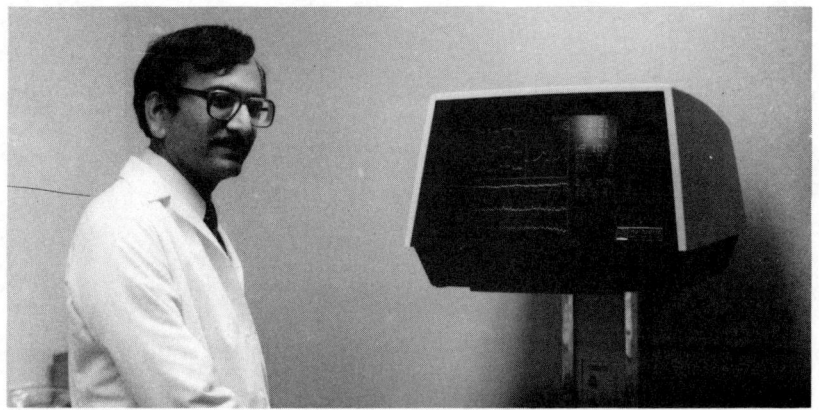

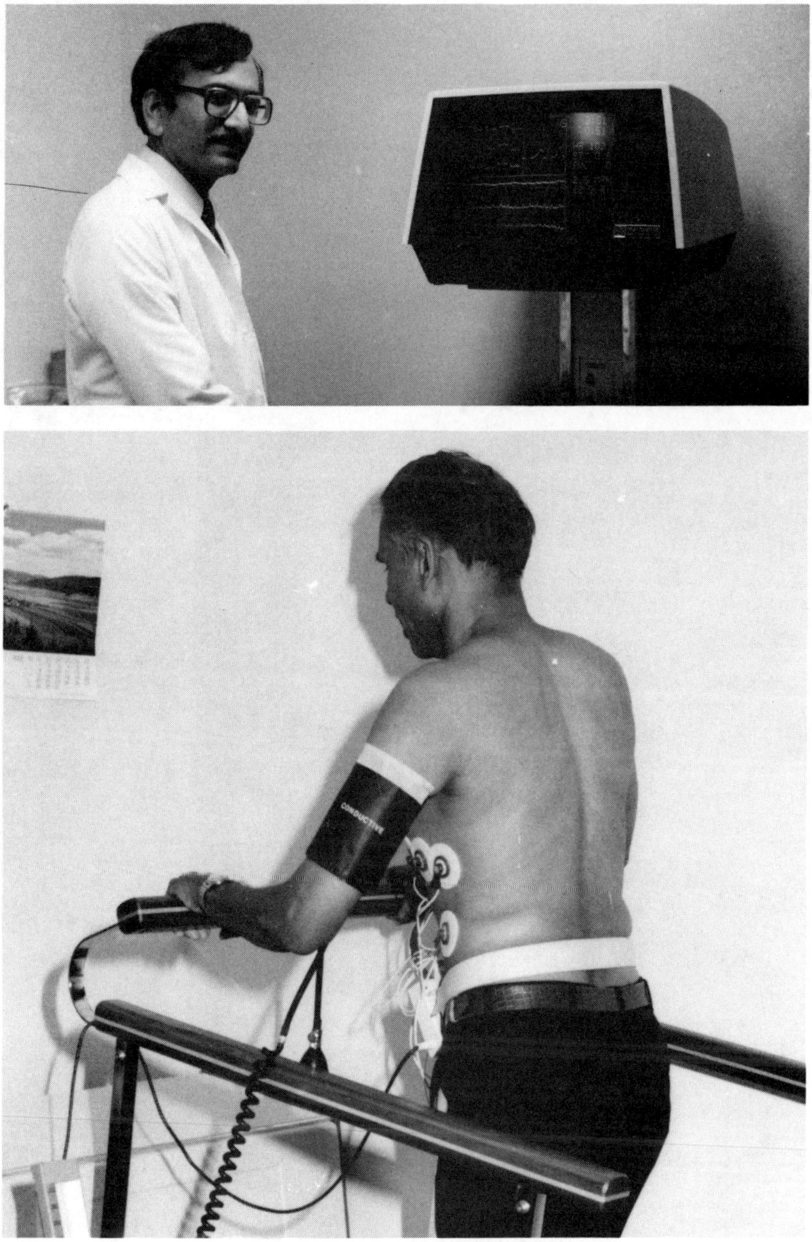

Figure 27. Treadmill stress test.

Chapter **11**

Step 2—Towards Mental Excellence and Positive Self-Image Through The Meditative 20 Minutes

"Self-acceptance means accepting and coming to terms with ourselves now, just as we are, with all our faults, weaknesses, shortcomings, errors, as well as our assets and strengths."

Dr. Maxwell Maltz
Author of *Psycho-cybernetics*

Step 2 aims at developing positive mental attitudes through contemplation, self-psychoanalysis, and other techniques so that a strong self-image can be built. The purpose is to acquire mastery over the emotional part of the mind and to reach a state of equanimity, so that the basic negative emotions—anger, fear, and grief—can be managed with appropriate response. Step 2 is called "the meditative 20 minutes" to indicate the minimum duration of time one should spend in a day directing one's attention inward of oneself. This chapter presents some of the proven techniques, which are easily practicable for the development of equanimity and a positive self-image.

Meaning of Meditation

The word "meditation" means different things to different people, and to many it brings a notion of mysticism and religious and spiritual involvement of some kind. However, it is not the notion for which it is employed here. It is used to mean all types of normal thought processes under the conscious control of the person, such as pondering, reflecting on, contemplating, planning or projecting in the mind, etc. Meditation implies that the thought process is taken beyond the realm of emotions so that the person's thinking is not clouded by his or her emotions. Because of the absence of the emotions during meditation, the brainwave pattern falls, in general, in the alpha range, indicating a state of deep relaxation of the body and mind, known as the "alpha state."

Many forms and levels or stages of meditation are possible along with different levels of mental awareness. Dreaming, visualization, autosuggestion, hypnosis, religious meditation, transcendental meditation and cosmic meditation are indicative of the different possible levels of conscious awareness, which the practitioner is capable of experiencing. Hence, meditation is also known as "the experiencing experience."

Meditation and Brain Waves
Beta State

Beta waves are associated with our waking state. Depending on the intensity of your mental state of excitement, the brain wave frequency varies from 13 cycles per second (CPS) and above. Beta wave pattern is of high frequency and low amplitude. Higher beta activity indicates that the person is in a mental state of hyperactivation under the influence of intense emotions such as anger or fear. Fury state and panic state are manifestive states when the fight or flight response has been evoked and the person is under intense emotional stress. Along with the high frequency brain activity, there follow the physiological changes of increase in heart beat rate, blood pressure and involuntary muscle tension and the like. Neuropsychologists and stress researchers have found that all stresses occur in the domain of high frequency beta waves, and that at lower frequencies a person becomes more relaxed.

Alpha State

When a person is in an unstressed state, slower wave length activity is seen in the Electroencephalograph (EEG). Alpha brain waves which form a low-frequency, high-amplitude pattern of 8 to 12 CPS are predominant during this relaxed, waking state. During this state the blood pressure returns to the normal value for that person, consistent with his physical blood circulation system. Alpha state is the most desirable waking state since the mind's cognitive and creative potentials are at their highest. Alpha state is a relaxed waking state.

Theta and Delta States

The transition stage between being awake and sleeping is marked by still slower brain waves of 4 to 7 CPS, called theta waves. It is usually a short period, lasting less than 10 minutes. Psychologist **P. G. Zimbardo** prefers to call this as Stage 1 sleep and considers it as the "hypnagogic" state. In this mental state reactivity to outside stimuli is reduced, thoughts drift, the anchor of reality is cast off and hallucinations arise. Also, during Stage 1 sleep rapid eye movements and dreaming occur. This is followed by Stage 2 sleep which is marked by bursts of brain waves that wax and wane.

Stage 3 is deep sleep. It is defined by EEG patterns of very slow frequency of one half to 3 CPS and very large amplitude (greater than 75 microvolts) known as delta waves. Stage 4 is considered as very deep sleep when the slowest of the delta waves occur. Figure 28 shows the various stages of bioorganic existence and the associated brain wave rhythms.

Place and Time for Meditation

Though meditation can be done literally at any place, it is desirable that you practice meditation in the privacy of your home or office away from the gaze of other people or in temples of worship meant for prayer and meditation. We are concerned here primarily with your physical safety, because during meditation your consciousness may tend to shift away from your immediate environment for a prolonged period of time, and as such you may become oblivious to any approaching danger. Hence, it is important that you ensure maximum safety to your person by choosing an appropriate place.

Central to meditation is an alert mind. Your choice of time for meditation should, therefore, be such that you will be able to stay awake and alert, depending on your nature of routines of daily living. Early morning and late evening hours are most suitable for most people. Meditation should not be done within two hours of any heavy meal for obvious reasons of avoiding drowsiness and falling asleep. Though meditation does not require any special clothing, loose fitting

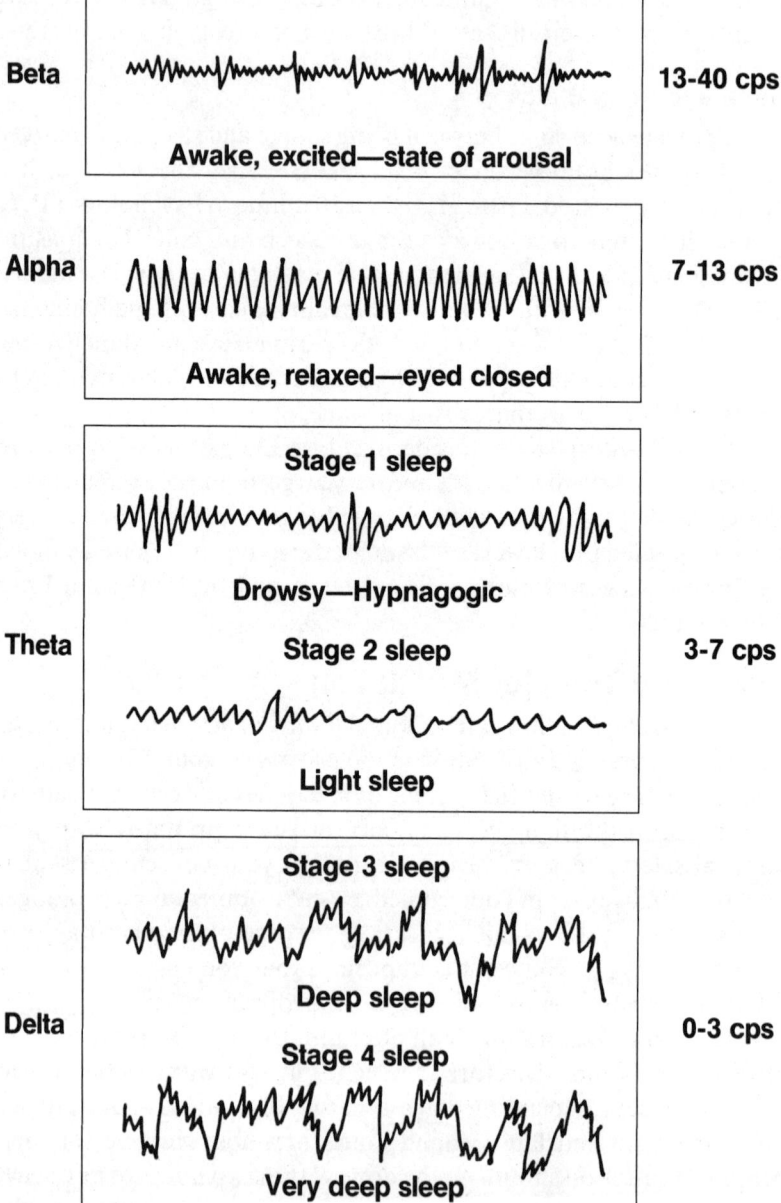

Figure 28. Brainwaves.

garments to ensure maximum physical comfort and to keep you warm enough in your chosen environment are recommended.

Meditation involves turning your attention from the external environment towards your inner awareness and tuning your mind to reach harmony with your inner forces. Hence, a quiet place with least external stimuli in the form of noise, smell and other disturbances is the most desirable. Mild incense has been found to soothe the hypothalamus, the neurocenter of the brain, to induce physical relaxation, the prerequisite for meditation. It is important that your meditation site is well ventilated without being unduly warm or cold.

It is important that your family members should respect your need to be alone during the meditative period and cooperate with you in keeping a quiet environment. It is recommended that you try to adhere strictly to the meditative practice carried out at the same time and place every day as a matter of self-discipline.

Posture and Procedure for Meditation

1. Choose a sitting position on the floor or in a straight-back chair that is most comfortable to you. Reclining and lying positions are not recommended for meditation as they may lead to a drowsy state of mind and sleep. See Figure 29.
2. Having comfortably seated, pay attention to your breathing. After a couple of deep diaphragmatic breaths, return to normal breathing. Close your eyes.
3. Keep your mind in a state of passivity with no violent emotions. Feelings of anger, fear, grief, and joy must be transcended, so that you feel fully relaxed.
4. With your eyes closed, fix your attention on the spot in your forehead between the two eye-brows. You may visualize a circle with a central dot to aid in focusing your inward gaze.
5. Stay passively, physically and mentally, in that position for about 5 minutes. Let non-emotional thoughts freely flow in your mind. You will feel the tensed muscles of your forehead beginning to relax. You are slowly reaching the alpha state of relaxation. You will feel it through the absence of muscle tension anywhere in your body.

118   SELF-EXCELLENCE

The stage is now set for your willful application of one or more of the following meditative techniques for building a strong self-image contributive to mental excellence.
1. Self-acceptance through autosuggestion
2. Contemplation
3. Self-psychoanalysis
4. Visualization

Figure 29. Meditative posture.

Self-Acceptance Through Autosuggestion

With your eyes closed in the meditative position, let your "I" consciousness, independent of your body and mind, project your "image"— that is "YOU"—, on your mental screen, so that you are able to see your faults, weaknesses, shortcomings, errors, as well as your assets and strengths, both physical and emotional. Now, that is your present "image". Accept this image in total in your mind. This suggestion of acceptance is taken by your subconscious mind. After about 15 minutes, open your eyes slowly. Stay relaxed for a couple of minutes before getting up and resuming your normal activities.

During your working hours the suggestion of the subconscious begins to act on your conscious mind. Repeat this self-acceptance drama in the stage of your mind during subsequent meditative sessions till you are totally comfortable at your image. This is the single most important step in your ascent towards self-excellence, because the very foundation of self-excellence rests on self-acceptance. Without self-acceptance there is no mental excellence.

Now, after a week's repetition or more, test the strength of your self-acceptance by what I call a "feel test". It is simply a matter of subjectively evaluating how you feel about yourself. If you felt more comfortable with yourself and your false feelings of inferiority disappeared, then you are on the right track. With true self-acceptance, the seed of self-confidence begins to germinate in your mind. The great plastic surgeon, **Dr. Maxwell Maltz,** wrote in his book, *Creative Living for Today,* that "your surest guide to success is your acceptance of yourself".

Self-acceptance acts like a powerful catalyst. It makes you feel more secure within yourself and provides a release for the accumulated strains due to the stressors in your life. Your worth as a human being suddenly increases in your eye, thus enhancing your self-esteem. You will not say "I hate myself" any more.

What does self-acceptance do to bring about such a drastic change in your living? You may remember from our earlier discussion that behind every stress is an unresolved conflict at the conscious or subconscious level of the mind. The conflicts at the conscious level are eliminated by the self-acceptance, and as **Robert McKain** puts it, "it helps you live with yourself and enables you to accept other people". The technique of coming to grips with the conflicts at the subconscious level of your mind is discussed elsewhere in this chapter.

Contemplation

Self-acceptance has prepared the ground for you to explore and uncover your hitherto unrealized, dormant potentials for successful living. This is accomplished through contemplation during your meditative sessions.

With your eyes closed in the meditative position, bring yourself to the alpha state of relaxation. Now, begin contemplating about man, the microcosm, and his place in the Universe, the macrocosm. After many sessions of contemplation you will be able to self-realize the potentials in you, not only for survival as any other living organism, but also for a self-directed creative living. The creative power of the intellect of your mind will become apparent to you. You will discover the uniqueness of yourself as a human being. It is up to you to mobilize the power of creativity in you and use it for your coordinated life plan for self-fulfillment.

Also, through contemplation, you must unearth the uniqueness characteristic of your own mind (see Chapter 2). In it lies your success potential. Small or large, your undertakings will be successful only if they are in tune with your mind's uniqueness characteristic. For this reason, it is very important that you become aware of this great asset of yours and try to reach for it through contemplation.

Self-Psychoanalysis

We mentioned before that through self-acceptance you will be able to eliminate the conflicts in your mind at the conscious level. However, the conflicts at the subconscious level need to be managed differently. It must be done through professional help if the conflict is deep-seated. Otherwise, self-help using psychoanalysis can be tried. Though many people think that one can not analyze and evaluate oneself in their behavioral responses, psychologists unanimously agree that self-evaluation is not only possible but is also the right course for enriching one's life.

With your eyes closed in the meditative position, bring yourself to the alpha state of relaxation. Pick up one event at a time from your behavioral pattern that bothers you every time. In the stage of your mind, reconstruct the same or similar events of the past, however unpleasant and uncomfortable they may be. View the scene objectively as if you are viewing the performance of a movie character on the screen and evaluate yourself in the scene to know how you reacted to those past events. Note your personality traits in those incidents. Analyze them and try to find which of the trait or traits is the cause of the conflict.

If you are able to objectively identify the source of the conflict, you can take steps for suitable modifications in your attitude and behavior in the future, so that no conflict is encountered in similar events. By repeatedly going through those events in your mind in your successive meditative sessions and matching them with your chosen attitude and behavior modifications, you will be able to minimize, if not entirely eliminate, the effects of the stressful conflicts.

It is important to note here that self-psychoanalysis, when properly applied, is a powerful tool at your disposal for attitude and behavior modification on your part to apply for future events. This in itself is "willful adaptation" at its best, and is logical after your attempt at self-acceptance. However, the whole concept is more easily said than done. It needs patience and perseverance on your part.

Visualization

Visualization is the process of forming mentally visual images of objects not present to the eye. It is an imagined scene with all its concreteness. It is most effective in the alpha state of relaxation when the mind is most receptive. It has the potential to use visual imagery to change the mental and physiological state through the power of positive suggestion. Visualization holds the key to unlock the higher reaches of one's own consciousness. Simple to learn and practice, it is the most effective of all the techniques for psychophysical relaxation and for building self-confidence.

When you create a vivid mental picture, your body actually responds to the visualization as if it were a real experience. **Dr. Maltz,** in his book, *Psycho-cybernetics,* mentions that your nervous system can not tell the difference between an imagined experience and a real experience. In either case, it acts automatically to the information you provide from your forebrain. Your nervous system reacts appropriately to what you visualize, thus establishing a psychophysical response to the visualized imagery.

Dr. Kenneth R. Pelletier, in his book, *Mind as Healer Mind as Slayer,* mentions that the induced visualization can be employed to stimulate the creative imagination, and when used while in a state of passive concentration, it is a very powerful tool to mobilize the resources of both the body and mind.

With your eyes closed in the meditative position, bring yourself to the alpha state of relaxation. Visualize yourself as a self-confident person in control of a winning situation in all its details. Hold the visualized image in your mind for about 15 minutes and live through the successful moments again and again. See Figure 30. Your nervous system reacts to the imagined input, and works positively increasing your self-esteem, and thereby the self-confidence.

On waking up, as a result of the many continued sessions of visualization, you will feel more confident, and your self-image grows stronger. In the same manner, you can effectively use visualization to impart yourself any desired positive mental attitude.

You can also use visualization for psychophysical relaxation at home or the office. Visualize yourself as a totally relaxed person enjoying the serenity of the secluded beach on the ocean front, your nervous system gets the message and conveys to the skeletal muscles to relax as if you were on the beach.

Other Benefits of Meditation

It is a medically verified fact now that during deep meditation blood pressure drops down due to psychophysical relaxation. Persons suffering from hypertension can make use of meditation to lower their blood pressure along with medically prescribed drugs without any side effects.

The cosmic connection between microcosmic man and the macrocosmic Universe is beyond the realm of mind's intellectual grasp and beyond words and expressions. It can only be self-realized through intuition transcending the very source of thought. Intuition

Figure 30. Visualization of Success.

as a source of knowledge without sensory perceptions can be reached only through deep meditation after disciplined conditioning of the body and mind.

Since the aspirant of cosmic wisdom starts by disciplining the body and mind, he or she will have a better control on many of the stress producing situations than others, primarily because of his or her changed perception of the society and the Universe, obtained through meditation.

Self-Actualization

Humanistic psychologist **Abraham Maslow** believed that there is a tendency in every human being toward *self-actualization,* which represents the constant striving to realize our inherent potentials for creativity and self-fulfillment. It is here that meditation has its most powerful impact on the individual. Since nobody else can release your potentials from the deep recess of your mind other than yourself, you have to take conscious effort for self-realization of those potentials. Meditation offers the key to "unlock the door to internal resources waiting to be released".

Emotion Management

We noted elsewhere that the onset of emotions in the mind sets in motion a range of complex brainwaves of varying intensity and wave length, besides activating the autonomic nervous system and the adrenal glands. It is our physical response under this emotional condition that constitutes the major element in our behavior pattern and personality traits. The management of emotions, then, undoubtedly plays a key role in mitigating the effects of emotional stress.

How to Handle Fear

Fear is partly a learned, yet partly an unlearned and innate response. It can be at your conscious level or at the subconscious. Fear of the unknown is the most common base of anxiety in us. Fear also has a survival potential in it, in that a conscious fear can make you alert and become more cautious. On the other hand, fear can be deadly. It can shock a person into inaction, paralyzing his or her ability to cope with realities of life. Fear being a basic human emotion can induce psychosomatic disturbances if not managed properly.

The most effective way to handle a conscious fear is rationalization. Analyzing the cause of the fear and charting out an action plan to meet the fear inducing situation is very effective when fear is well defined. Talking out your fears to a trusted friend, doctor or a clergyman will take the edge off the fear and help you to take positive actions and countermeasures.

Resorting to alcohol and drugs to drown your fears and anxieties is temporary escapism. It is not only cowardly and foolish, but will aggravate the stress in the long run.

Subconscious fear usually takes the form of various phobias and subliminal behavior. A person suffering from any kind of phobia will do well to get professional help rather than living through the stress in a state of mental and physical discomfort.

Fear of making mistakes, fear of not being able to meet dead lines, and fear of social disapproval are among the most common fears which produce stress overload to most people. Accepting one's limitations and taking a realistic attitude will certainly reduce the impact of such anxiety inducing fears.

How to Handle Anger

Anger occurs when one's self-concept, his beliefs, standards and expectations are threatened, implying a challenge to his values. Those who feel less secure with themselves often become angry easily. Becoming angry is one thing and reacting under anger is another. It is the latter that needs to be consciously guarded, and effort is needed to defuse the anger without having any detrimental effect to oneself or to the interpersonal relationship with others.

The best way to handle anger is to allow some time to elapse before you react verbally or physically from the instant when you become consciously angry. The person involved in the event provoking your anger may be someone you know, such as a family member or an associate in the office or a total stranger. By taking a few deep breaths or simply counting to twenty mentally, you gain time for a thought-out reaction rather than a spontaneous outburst against that person.

Remember that everytime you become angry, your blood pressure goes up and your adrenal gland emits the stress hormone adrenaline into your blood stream. You may recall their effects on your physical system which we discussed earlier.

Another simple but effective measure in controlling anger is a mirror biofeed technique. Keep a small mirror handy on your office table and at your home. Whenever you get angry or tensed up, make it a point to look at your face in the mirror and try to bring out a smile before you react verbally or otherwise. Since smile is possible only when your brain produces alpha waves associated with relaxation, your anger which occurs in the realm of beta waves, will be overcome by your own smile. Since it is impossible to genuinely smile and be angry at the same time, smile becomes a powerful antidote to anger. Also, once you see the contortions of your facial appearance under the spell of anger and remember how you are seen by other people, you will realize what anger does to you externally and internally. You will also realize the power of your own smile in overcoming anger.

Pouring your anger in words on a piece of paper in the form of a letter to the person who invoked your anger and tearing it off is also an effective means of ventilating your emotional feelings. For centuries meditation has been known to be an effective weapon against anger.

How to Handle Grief

Emotional stress arising out of deep personal loss, such as the death of a spouse, a deeply loved relative or a friend, a catastrophic business collapse or the loss of a job on which family sustenance is dependent is highly subjective in its impact on the individual. A sense of hopelessness, feeling of despair and detachment are the various stages that are likely to follow. It is rather difficult to prescribe a counter measure against grief. However, the general rule of "accept and adapt" is the best way to manage a grief-provoking situation or event, leaving the rest to time—the healer of wounds.

Desensitization

Since anxiety arising from undefined emotional stress and fear is a major factor in preventing a person from being at peace with oneself and causing an inability to approach positive goals, mental relaxation becomes difficult till the cause of the anxiety is identified and overcome. Psychologist **Joseph Wolpe** developed a reciprocal inhibition technique, called systematic desensitization, based on the notion that it is difficult to be both happy and sad, or relaxed and anxious, at the same time. The method involves in identifying the stimuli that provoke anxiety, arranging them in a hierarchy ranked from the weakest to strongest, and systematically deal with them in vivid visualization after a training of progressive muscle relaxation.

This is akin to a mental rehearsal of the stress provoking event in its entirety, but step by step, in a state of psychological relaxation. The subconscious is thus introduced to the would-be stimuli, thereby training it to be able to confidently meet and respond to the actual stimuli later on. Since your nervous system can not tell the difference between an imagined and a real stimulus, it can be trained to respond in a predetermined manner that is most appropriate for you without being unduly stressed emotionally. Desensitization works best when visualization and physiological relaxation go hand in hand in each imagined step. It has been successfully applied to a diversity of human problems, including generalized fears such as stage fright, examination anxiety, sex problems and a variety of day-to-day stress provoking events.

Though desensitization was originally devised as a clinical method needing the help of a therapist, it is ideally suited as a self-help technique to effect mental relaxation. It is an effective tool in the management of emotional stress and meeting the challenges of daily living.

Desensitization Exercise

Sit in a quiet place in a comfortable posture. Breathe slowly and steadily, paying attention to your incoming and outgoing breath. Close your eyes. Identify the real-life event which is causing you mental distress and which you want to overcome.

Now distract yourself mentally and concentrate on relaxing yourself physiologically through breathing and bring yourself to the alpha state of relaxation. When you are deeply relaxed, mentally return back to the event you had isolated for desensitization. Visualize the event in a step by step manner, such that each successive step is more stressful in nature. Visualize the first step in your hierarchy which is the least stress provoking and see if you are relaxed. If so, move on to the next step. However, if you feel tension in your muscles in the first step, stop imagining the event and concentrate on becoming totally relaxed again.

As you become physically relaxed, return to the step you had temporarily left. Since your nervous system had already an input, this time you may not be as anxious as before. If you are relaxed and comfortable with that step, move on to the next step of the feared event. In this manner, attempt to advance further in your hierarchy, getting closer and closer to visualizing the actual event while remaining calm and relaxed. The more accurate your visualization of the hierarchial circumstances of the event, the more effective the desensitization will be. It may take more than one session to get complete control of your psychophysical balance. In spite of the desensitization training, there can be a little more tension associated with the real event when you actually encounter it.

The Relaxation Response

Recently **Dr. Herbert Benson** of the Harvard Medical School figured out that to maintain the homeostasis of bioorganisms there is an innate physiologic response that is diametrically different from the stress response. This natural and innate response serves as the protective mechanism against "overstress" to mitigate and counter the effects of the fight-or-flight response. Benson found that this response, acting through the body's autonomic or involuntary system, causes a reduction in the activity of the sympathetic nervous system bringing down the heart rate, blood pressure, rate of breathing and metabolism. He called this the "Relaxation Response." He and his team of investigators found that the Relaxation Response is easily and readily amenable for evocation for all people with some training. It can be used as a prevention against stress-related ailments and to induce deep relaxation of the body and mind.

Relaxation Response Exercise

In his book, *The Relaxation Response,* **Dr. Benson** presents the technique developed at Thorndike Memorial Laboratory and Boston's Beth Israel Hospital to evoke the Relaxation Response. An understanding of the following four components is essential before you attempt the exercise program.

(1) A Quiet Environment
   This is primarily to ensure as minimum outside distractions as possible. A quiet room or a place of worship is suitable.

(2) A Mental Device
   Since you are going to turn your attention introspectively, you need an aid for concentration which may be in the form of a sound or a word. Since the major difficulty is "mind wandering," the repetition of the word or phrase is a way to help break the train of distracting thoughts. Pay attention to the normal rhythm of breathing which enhances the effect of the repetition of the sound or the word.

(3) A Passive Attitude
   You should let your mind cast away all anxieties and worries about mundane problems. It is normal and natural to have distracting thoughts. Do not worry about them, but let them drift away leaving you with a passive inward attention. The passive attitude is the most important element in eliciting the Relaxation Response.

(4) A Comfortable Position
   A comfortable posture free from undue muscular tension is needed to maintain the physiological relaxation during the exercise program. Sitting positions are preferable since there is a tendency to fall asleep if you are lying down.

The Technique

(1) Sit quietly in your chosen comfortable position in a state of passivity.

(2) Breathe normally and close your eyes.

(3) Mentally concentrate at your feet muscles and slowly relax them. Proceed relaxing your muscles up to your face, till you feel no tension anywhere in your body.

(4) Turn your attention on your breathing. As you breathe out, say the word, "ONE," silently or just audibly to yourself. Now, keep repeating breathing in and out with the utterance of "ONE" along with the out-breath. Fix your attention on the sound of "ONE."

(5) Continue for about 20 minutes, maintaining the passive attitude and the bodily relaxation. When distracting thoughts occur, gently ignore them by concentrating on the sound "ONE," now rhythmically sounding along with your out-breathing.
(6) Set aside a specific time and practice the technique once or twice daily before meals. Consistency in practice promotes the elicitation of the Relaxation Response.

The Relaxation Response and the Alpha State

Dr. Benson's research showed that the regular elicitation of the Relaxation Response retards the activity of the sympathetic nervous system to bring down oxygen consumption, heart rate, respiratory rate, and blood pressure. Subsequent biofeedback researchers observed that the regular practice of the Relaxation Response aids to achieve deep relaxation of both body and mind. **Maxwell Cade** and **Nona Coxhead** have indicated in their book, *The Awakened Mind,* that the Relaxation Response promotes self-awareness and increases self-control. EEG measurements seem to indicate that during the occurrence of the Relaxation Response the brain wave rhythms range from 8 to 13 cycles per second, indicating a predominant alpha state of conscious awareness. Complete absence of beta waves (higher than 13 CPS) indicates the physiological relaxation associated with this state of being.

Chapter 12

Step 3—Towards Goal-Achieving Excellence Through The Creative 20 Minutes

"Extensive research shows consistent patterns in the work lives of so-called goal seekers. These people exhibit confidence; they are action-minded and expect to win. ... They feel a strong need to tackle tough goals and achieve them, not just well but with excellence. They set long and short-range goals for themselves and plan their lives ahead."

Charles L. Hughes
Author of *Goal Setting*

Desire for creative excellence is innate in human beings and is dormant in every one of us. It blossoms and manifests itself through the intellect-part of the mind under proper conditions. The created manifestation can be mental such as the visualization of a scenery in all its vivid details, or it can be physical such as a beautifully constructed palace, or the creation of a symphony. It can also be the goals in life and their achievement, because goals need to be created and visualized by the individual before seeking their achievement. Since a sense of satisfaction and fulfillment accompanies all achievements, however humble they may be, it is obvious that you live best and get the most out of your living only when your life is planned and goal-oriented.

Step 3 aims at developing your creative potential and making use of it to achieve the goals, which you might set for yourself in your personal and professional life. Step 3 is called "the creative 20 minutes" to indicate the minimum duration of time one should spend in a day developing the skills needed for achieving goals. In this chapter are presented the principles of goal-setting and the laws of success that lead to the fruition of the desired goals.

Principles of Goal Setting

In Chapter 8 we mentioned that assigning a purpose to your living introduces new meaning to your life and that your very thought processes will reorient themselves to align your actions on a course towards the purpose. The purpose constitutes a long-range objective, and hence you need an action plan to systematically take you step by step towards the realization of the purpose. Each step in the action plan is a goal to be surmounted. Thus, you need many coordinated goals, to form a part of the masterplan and your life itself becomes goal-oriented. You can take on any number of different purposes and their goals simultaneously, if you can manage.

Goals Must Be Well Defined

For a goal to be achievable, it must have three characteristics: a well-defined objective, a measurable target, and a specified time frame. Absence of any one of these three will reduce the goal to the level of only a good intention. Intentions don't take anyone anywhere. Goals must not be too rigid either. They must be flexible enough to accommodate changes and modifications, but rigid enough to produce measurable results. Above all, goals must be realistic.

It is essential that working towards a goal must be enjoyable to you. If it is not enjoyable, the goal is not worth achieving; change to a new goal.

Goals Must Be Interrelated

For your individual and personal goals to be meaningful, they must be interrelated to those of your professional goals, goals of other members of the family, and your social and vacation goals. Once the goals are well-defined and delineated, you should concentrate on one at a time until you achieve the objective of that goal. However, it is better if you can organize your goals into three groups: immediate goals, short-range goals, and long-range goals. In this lies the secret of goals management.

Immediate Goals

Immediate goals concern themselves with things to be done for the day and within the week. It is very important that you realize the fact that you live only one day at a time. In order to get the most out of this one day, you must organize a "5 minute strategy-planning" at the beginning of the day to get started and evaluate your activities at the end of the day before going to sleep in a "5 minute strategy-review" session.

I can not over-emphasize the power of these 2 brief sessions in your life in making things happen for you when practiced as a routine. After all, your future life is nothing else but the sum total of all single days ahead of you, and your goal achievement is the sum total of all the effects of the daily and weekly achievements. Weekly goals organized on the same pattern as the daily goals can take care of fluctuations and deviations that might happen during the week, without losing the direction.

Daily goals lend meaning to the routine chores of the day without inducing a feeling of boredom, be it at home or the place of work. You will be amazed at the amount of things you can do in a single working day, when you had begun it with a "5 minute strategy planning." For greater effectiveness, put your strategy on paper in writing in a list of activities, prioritied for the day, and keep it right in front of you for periodic perusal.

Short-Term Goals

Whereas daily and weekly goals in effect constitute the action part, the direction and objective are provided by the goal set in a meaningful distant horizon. Short-term goals are ideal for the achievement of many worthwhile things in both personal and professional life. Goals set within a time frame of one to 3 years can be considered as a short-term goal. Buying a car, working on a college degree, going on a long family vacation, putting through a professional deal, starting a new business, etc., can all be set within a meaningful time frame of 3 years.

Once the goal is set, visualize the action plan to get you there on time. The principles of success or the achievement of a goal are presented elsewhere in this chapter. Using these principles, you should formulate a daily and weekly action plan, breaking the short-term goal into many manageable elementary goals, amenable for achievement.

Remember that you are not a machine set on a goal-seeking mission. Don't forget your human sensitivity. It is not just the goal, but the very process of reaching the goal is a part of your living. It must be enjoyable to you,—lock, stock, and barrel—the working towards the goal, small achievements on the way, and finally the goal itself. Once the goal is reached, relish and share your enjoyment with family and friends. What counts is not the magnitude of the goal, but the feeling of self-fulfillment, the elation of creative living, the lingering fragrance of self-excellence.

Long-Term Goals

Buying a home, building a steady retirement income, an unhurried global tour, and goals of this nature can be called long-term goals, considering the lengthy duration of the time frame needed for their fruition. Uncrystallized ideas and wishes do not constitute long-term goals. They will remain as wishes, and wishes do not take you anywhere.

The action plan for a long-term goal is similar to that of a short-term plan, but with a greater freedom for changes and modifications. From an achievement point of view, a long-term goal can be broken into a series of short-term goals, executed and periodically evaluated on the long time frame.

Keep Record of Progress

It is essential that you keep a written record of your goals, and their periodic progress for systematic evaluation. Your progress will depend on the feedback you get from the results. Also, the written records eliminate the guess work, and make you realize where you stand with reference to your original objective. It will help you make effective changes and modifications, and redefine the goals, if needed. Once the goals are well defined, motivation is essential for their achievement.

3 Elements of Motivation

The three elements of motivation leading to success are:
1. belief in yourself and in your goals
2. desire to achieve
3. desire to excel.

Few people realize that the success or achievement of their goals is mostly dependent on themselves. Many attribute it to luck and factors extraneous to themselves. They are quick to blame their bosses and environment for their failure. You may remember that we mentioned before about the uniqueness characteristic of individuals. If your goal is in tune with your uniqueness characteristic, you will be naturally motivated to achieve and excel in that direction, and this is the secret of success. Of course, it is for you to self-realize your uniqueness characteristic through subjective self-examination as we had discussed elsewhere in this book.

Stumbling Blocks to Success

The following factors constitute the major stumbling blocks preventing success:
1. Fear of failure
2. Failure attitude
3. Lack of motivation
4. Ill-defined goals
5. Lack of faith in the objective
6. Lack of incentive
7. Lack of self-discipline

People often fail in reaching their goals because they have a lurking fear of failure and an unwillingness to face it. Seldom do they realize that failure is a stepping stone to success and that their continued effort will take them to their goal. They mistake an unsuccessful attempt as a calamity, and their self-image is not strong enough to accept failure with grace and move on. It is easy not to fail by not trying, and that is the path they take. The second major reason is a failure attitude. The person believes that he can never succeed. Unless he dehypnotizes himself out of this attitude, as **Dr. Maxwell Maltz** puts it, he can not turn on his built-in success-machine. How can you win, when you have programmed yourself to lose!

The third reason why people don't succeed is a lack of motivation. Without adequate motivation, the desire to achieve and excel can not be kindled in a person. Motivation acts as a propelling force, pushing the person along an action course of success. Also, often people fail, though adequately motivated, due to ill-defined nature of the goals such as when the time frame is unrealistic or when the goal is not clearly measurable.

Lack of faith in the objective is another cause of failure, particularly in group projects, where more than one person is involved. When a goal is thrust on a group—as often happens in industrial complexes and when the group members do not have faith in the objective, goal-achievement will only be a myth. Lack of incentive is yet another reason why success is unachievable in many situations. Since human beings act on self-interest, there must be something satisfactory to them in achieving the goal, either monetarily, emotionally, or otherwise.

The last but the most important factor preventing success in any undertaking is the lack of self-discipline needed to carry out the action part of the planning. Motivation and self-discipline go generally hand in hand. Adequate motivation induces the physical and mental conditioning needed in a person for self-discipline to work towards the goal. However, if self-discipline is impaired for any reason, success tends to become elusive.

The 7 Laws of Success

The following seven "laws" have been generally recognized as the basis for success in any venture or goal-seeking mission.
1. Keep the objective at sight
2. Keep studying about the goal
3. Make adequate preparation
4. Work with enthusiasm
5. Be ready for due sacrifice
6. Do not mind others
7. Get continuous feedback

Keeping the objective at the top level of your mind at all times during working towards a goal is the first and foremost thing to remember. It acts as a catalyst mobilizing your thoughts and actions and steering them towards your objective. It should be followed by a continuing effort on your part to learn everything possible within your limitations about the goal you seek. This study helps to bring to light the nature of the road ahead, the impediments on the way, the pitfalls to be aware of, and above all, your own shortcomings relative to the goal.

The next step is to make preparations on your part. This is, in effect, to get control over the prerequisites compatible to the objective and the goal. Many a person fail in their ventures, not for lack of hard work but because of overlooking the need to get the prerequisites mastered in the first place. With prerequisites taken care of, now only you are actually ready to embark on the action part of the goal-seeking game. **Abraham Lincoln** said that success is 99% perspiration and 1% inspiration. Motivated, consistent, and systematic work in your project is called upon now. It is not the kind of drudgery of the sullen workaholic, but the excellence of an enthusiastic executive.

It is inevitable that a certain amount of sacrifice of your personal time and comforts is called upon in the achievement of any worthwhile goal. There is no compromise on this fact. However, an enthusiastic goal-seeker does not even consider it as a sacrifice because for him or her it becomes a way of life—not thrust upon, but willingly adopted. While the opinions of others whom you live and work with count, you should not pay attention to any discouraging or distracting comment about your goal. We mentioned before that your faith in yourself and in your objective is the seed of success, and you should learn to discount the opinions of others not founded on facts.

Finally, getting continuing and periodic feedback about the results of your effort on a measureable scale is a necessary condition for success. An evaluation of the feedback lets you know how well you are doing relative to your objective and the time frame. It lets you decide to have changes and modifications in the approach and nature of execution, if needed. Periodic evaluation of the feedback serves as both a monitoring and a warning device. It is the forerunner of what is yet to come. Its message is loud and clear for the goal seeker. When any goal, small or big, short-range or long-range is tackled systematically in accordance with these seven laws, the chances of achieving the goal are very high.

Creative Techniques

"The Creative 20 minutes" can be applied to the following techniques, which, in turn, will contribute to the development of creative excellence in your chosen field of interest:
1. Visualization
2. Skill-learning
3. Overlearning
4. Role-playing

Visualization

As we had discussed before, visualization is the process of forming mentally visual images of objects not visible to the eye. With your eyes closed, bring yourself to the alpha state of relaxation.

Create the project that you are planning as your goal in your mind's eye, and visualize the whole project from the beginning to the end. Examine part by part looking at the details that need to be worked out in your waking hours. This examination will show you where your weakness lies in not understanding or in your lack of something. In your waking hours you can attend to them, thus progressing a little towards the desired goal.

I used this technique effectively for the project of writing and publishing this book in your hand. I visualized step by step every aspect of writing and publishing and started working on the details during my waking hours, slowly but steadily. Repeated visualization of this project had created the image of the completed book in my mind with all the chapters duly organized long before it went to press.

You could use this technique for any of your planned creations, such as painting, piano-playing, building a home, or a complicated electronic circuitry. What matters is the consistent application of "the creative 20 minutes" principle to your planning project.

Skill-Learning

As the name indicates, you use "the creative 20 minutes" to learn a new skill, which you might have set as your new goal. Remember that this is a new skill that you are after, and as such learning may be slow in the beginning. Since it is your choice, it should be of interest and enjoyment to you. Consistent practice will soon make you proficient in your learning and take you towards your goal slowly but steadily.

I would like to point out that this is not a hobby. A hobby is an activity which you pursue at your leisure time primarily for your enjoyment, and not necessarily towards any goal. The purpose of "the creative 20 minutes" is goal-oriented and, therefore, is applied to the activity with consistency and a sense of commitment.

Overlearning

Overlearning is defined as the process of continued study or practice after reaching a criterion level of performance. Almost all accomplished musicians, artists, and other skilled people keep overlearning to be in top shape. You can also use this technique successfully for your developed skill for sheer enjoyment and relaxation during your "creative 20 minutes."

Role-Playing

Remember that you are a human being, first and last. All other forms of seeing yourself such as an executive, office manager, teacher, doctor, salesman, etc., are only role-playing. To play these roles, either you have been trained, or you have trained yourself.

If your goal is to become the president of a company, it simply means that you have to play the role of the company president. In order to prepare you for this new role, you can effectively use "the creative 20 minutes" for a session of visualization, in which you visualize yourself as the president. You think and act as the president whom you want to be, and this acting has the potential to induce in you the feeling of being a president. In other words, you are trying to create a successful future role by acting it out now. Though a fantasy at this time, it has the power to enhance your self-confidence and strengthen your self-image.

Some Worthwhile Long-Range Goals

Time frame: 5 years or more
1. Building or buying a home
2. Building a steady retirement income

3. World tour
4. Writing a book or a memoir
5. Owning a company
6. Active involvement in a social club, community affairs, or a church.

Some Worthwhile Short-Range Goals

Time frame: 3 years
1. Buying a car
2. Family vacation
3. Community involvement
4. Continuing education
5. Getting a college degree
6. Changing job
7. Changing residence
8. Building a bank balance
9. Losing a desired amount of body weight
10. Learning a new skill

Chapter 13

Step 4—Towards Excellence In Interpersonal Relations

> "If, as a result of reading this book, you get only one thing—an increased tendency to think always in terms of the other person's point of view, and see things from his angle as well as your own—if you get only that one thing from this book, it may easily prove to be one of the milestones of your career."
>
> **Dale Carnegie**
> Author of *How to Win Friends and Influence People*

One of the most stressful aspects of living for most people is in dealing with other people. It may be in one's own home, place of work, or elsewhere. Some people are easy to get along with whereas some others are difficult. Even the best of human relations to start with such as two people in love with each other can turn sour and end up in heart-breaking agony. On the other hand, what starts as a casual acquaintance many a time leads to a long-standing and meaningful tie and friendship between two people. Step 4 aims at understanding the dynamics of interpersonal relationship, the single most important factor in the lives of people living in organized societies such as ours, which are designed for purposeful human interactions for the welfare of all concerned. To be able to interact with others with least stress and without being a stressor to others is undoubtedly a desirable quality for a person striving for self-excellence.

Interpersonal Relationship and Stress

The stress of dealing with a difficult boss in the office, or an unfriendly neighbor or a quarrelsome spouse at home is the same as far as its impact on the person is concerned. It kindles the negative emotions of anger, fear or grief in varying degrees, though the circumstances may be different in each case. If the stressors persist over a long period of time, the physiological responses such as tension headaches, sleeplessness, and other stress-related symptoms are bound to occur. In other words, the human relationships in these cases are totally unpleasant and are contrary to happy and creative living.

The question, then, is: are there ways and means of interacting with other people effectively and efficiently and at the same time preventing unpleasant outcome in the relationship? In spite of the fact that behavior is a complex phenomenon, many psychologists think so. However, their concurrence of opinion implies that the person understands himself and others in the behavioral plane. Though there are set rules, regulations, and codes of ethics with reference to outward behavior, the emotional response of a person is beyond man-made restrictions. Interpersonal relationship is not a mechanistic process; it is inseparably mixed with spontaneous emotions. Human interactions and emotions go hand in hand. In spite of all the complexities, the following seven "laws" in the realm of human behavior seem to govern most interpersonal relationship.

7 Laws of Human Behavior

1. People act (behave) at their own self interest.
2. People like to be recognized and accepted as they are.
3. People act better-motivated on their own decisions rather than the decisions of others.
4. Cognitive and affective (rational and emotional) elements in human behavior are inseparable.
5. People with a positive self-image have the potential for emotional stability and meaningful human relations.
6. People who see purpose in their living are goal-oriented. Positive goals provide positive directions to their approach to life in general, and to their interpersonal relations in particular. Negative goals provide the opposite.

7. There is an innate, latent element of fondness or dislike (attraction or repulsion) in every person for the other person. This element evolves into a distinct feeling for the other person in interpersonal relationship reinforced by the emotional experiences in their behavioral interaction.

An understanding of these behavioral "laws" will help you to understand your own and other people's behavior and relationships to some extent. It can also help you to formulate a least stress behavioral pattern with your spouse and children at home, peers, bosses, and subordinates in the place of work, and with neighbors, friends and strangers elsewhere.

Humanistic psychologist **Carl Rogers** emphasized that good interpersonal relations are built on "a desire to understand empathetically, to really stand in the client's shoes, and to see the world from his vantage point." The basic undercurrent in interpersonal relations is human sensitivity, that is, a genuine respect for the feelings of the other person.

Though it is very difficult to pinpoint precisely the principles of good interpersonal relations, the following seven principles have been found to be the most universal. They are cultivable by any person with a genuine interest in developing self-excellence.

7 Principles of Interpersonal Relations

1. Caring and sharing
2. Catharsis
3. Respectful listening
4. Consulting in decision making
5. Smile and handshake
6. Sincere rewards
7. Don't hurt the self-esteem

Caring and Sharing

A smooth human relation is not possible between two persons or a group of people without the individuals showing a genuine concern for the others. Caring for the physical and mental wellbeing of the other person implies that you place the other person's interest ahead of yours and then work out a balance. This giving-in on your part draws the other person closer to you. A law of return in the psychological plane seems to work which states that people are compelled to give what they get.

How do you expect someone to care for you and listen to you, whether it is in your own home or office, if you don't have a sense of care and respect for that person? The moment "I don't care" attitude sets in, the relationship is heading for trouble and becomes a source of stress. It is here that attitudinal modification (AM) and behavioral modification (BM) on your part become your powerful tools of preventive and creative stress management.

Caring also means forgiving the faults of the other person and accepting the person as a whole. Acceptance provides the ideal climate for better interpersonal communication in the home or office and makes the other person more receptive to your ideas.

Caring also means sharing. It implies that you are willing to share your knowledge and assets to a degree meaningful to the relationship and environment. In office relationships this factor will win for you many friends among your peers and loyal support from subordinates. Without a sense of caring and sharing, all other interpersonal communication techniques are meaningless.

Catharsis

Catharsis means expressing oneself verbally to a willing listener in unrestrained terms his or her fears, anxieties and frustrations. In stressful situations the person feels emotional relief after talking out the problem. The idea has been known to mankind for a long time, and it has been in effective use in many cultures around the world. In fact, **Freud's** psychoanalysis is based on this concept.

In his book, *The Manager's Guide to Interpersonal Relations,* psychologist **Donald Sanzotta** recognizes the beneficial role of catharsis in what he calls as "therapeutic management". Catharsis has tremendous preventive potential in defusing stresses in day-to-day stressful situations both in the home and office. The unconscious mind is like a pressure cooker. It needs a release when the pressure becomes excessive. In humans the release can be obtained through verbalization and any creative activity.

In your relationship with others, you should watch out for opportunities to let the other person have the catharsis. Your ability to respond to catharsis in interpersonal relationship is a skill that can be developed just like any other skills. If you happen to be the one who needs catharsis, by all means do it, but with caution. Choose a trustworthy person whom you can depend on in unloading your pent-up feelings.

Respectful Listening

Ability to listen is an index of psychological maturity of an individual. It is a powerful tool in helping to establish effective communication between two or more people. However, few people realize the importance of being a good listener in the company of others. Highly successful executives in the business world are invariably great listeners.

Your becoming an effective listener depends on your paying attention to the following points:

1. Be concerned, look concerned and try to hear every word of the speaker. The speaker sees your face and you don't. Your face is the mirror of your mind, and you don't fool anyone but yourself trying to fake listening.
2. Make it a 2-way communication by intercepting the speaker with an appropriate question or agreeable remarks now and then to show him that you are following with interest and concern what he is saying. The more you agree during your listening, the closer the speaker moves towards you in his mind.
3. Don't be tempted to think what to say next. Wait till the speaker concludes whatever he wanted to say, giving him the feeling that he has conveyed his mind to you. This generates, as **Robert McKain** calls it, the "we" feeling, which is bound to win you his support and friendship.

Consulting in Decision Making

Good interpersonal relationship develops when people feel that they are a part of the decision making process. They are happy when they are consulted, even when they do not have a direct input. It is a behavioral trait that people are drawn closer consciously or subconsciously towards those who induce in them a happy and pleasant feeling by words or deeds. An executive or a manager in the office environment can take advantage of this human characteristic by consulting with the others in the group even through short personal meetings. The members of the group are more likely to go along with the leader, if they felt that they were consulted, even when the former had a predecided notion.

This principle works equally well in the home front. When the spouse and teen-age children feel that they are consulted on domestic issues, they are more likely to agree to your propositions. Being consulted by another person is a tremendous ego-booster to the individual, which enhances the later's self-esteem. Playing on the self-esteem of the other person is the key to effective interpersonal relationship.

Smile and Handshake

"Smile and the world smiles with you" is a familiar song that has a message for interpersonal relationship. There is no match for a genuine smile in warming up the other person's heart in this entire world, and come to think of it, there is an unlimited free supply of it dormant in your heart waiting to be released. And yet, how often do you use it voluntarily?

Smile is the physical manifestation of the pleasant emotional state of the mind. It is generally referred to a happy or joyous state. When negative emotions of fear, anger or grief are present, it is impossible to smile. Nothing is more obvious to others than a faked smile! Smile implies that you accept the other person as a whole, at least at that instant. We mentioned earlier in this chapter that one of the laws of human behavior is that people like to be recognized and accepted as they are. For this reason, your smile creates a pleasant environment for the interpersonal relationship. It may be with one person or a group.

There is more to smile than its being an index of the state of your mind. Research by neuropsychologists indicates that during the period of a genuine smile the brain cells undergo complex chemical changes in them. The brain generates alpha electrical waves and produces a chemical known as endorphin. The nature of endorphin is not yet fully understood, but its contribution to the physiological wellbeing is well known. Also, we have mentioned before that the alpha rhythm is an index of the relaxation of the body and mind.

Do not overlook the age-old hearty handshake and its role in building a positive interpersonal relationship. Handshakes relieve the tension in meeting strangers and provide warmth and affection in meeting old friends. The combination of a warm handshake and a genuine smile forms a strong foundation for any professional relationship. Their role in a creative stress management program can not be overemphasized.

Rewards

Good interpersonal relations are founded on mutually shared pleasant feelings between two or more people in their day-to-day interactions. This is true whether it is in the home or in the place of work. It is important that you recognize this fact in building and maintaining a good interpersonal relationship anywhere with those with whom you come into contact.

Considerate "rewards" or what psychologists call as "reinforcements" appropriate to the situation have been found to help in maintaining and enhancing the relationship. These rewards can be:
1. words of appreciation
2. written notes of thanks
3. raise in salary
4. promotions
5. gifts
6. entertaining at a dinner

These "rewards," however small or trivial they may appear, have the power to kindle the pleasant feelings of the receiver.

Your ability to show the other person how much you appreciate him or her is considered **by Dale Carnegie,** the author of *How to Win Friends and Influence People,* as the single most important skill in all human relations. However, the appreciation must not be confused with flattery. The former is sincere and comes out from the heart; the latter is insincere and comes from the teeth. One is unselfish; the other selfish.

Don't Hurt the Self-Esteem

The perfect human being is yet to be born. To err is human, and people will make mistakes in personal and professional lives. This fact must be kept foremost in view in any interpersonal relationship. How do you handle them? The key is to let the person know of the mistake without hurting his or her self-esteem. Criticizing the person for having made the mistake is the worst mistake you will ever make. Blunt criticism and direct confrontation, particularly in front of other people, has such a devastating effect on the person's self-image that he or she will be emotionally aroused, shaking the interpersonal relationship to the core. **Dale Carnegie** refers to this way of dealing with people the surest approach to make enemies.

If you must criticize, do it in private with the person, giving him or her a chance to save face. Criticism should not be angry verbalization on the part of the critic. It is intended only to point out and correct mistakes. Such a constructive criticism is good for the criticized and for the organization. It is constructive only when the criticized comes out without any resentment and emotional ill-feeling.

On the same token, if you are wrong, be quick to accept it. It takes courage and self-confidence to admit that you are wrong. When you accept, be bold to say sorry and ask to be forgiven. Nothing caters to the ego and self-esteem of a person more than finding himself or herself in a forgiving position. It provides a positive reinforcement to the interpersonal relationship, be it at home or in the place of work.

Other Aspects of Interpersonal Relationship
Assertiveness

Much has been said and written about the need to be assertive. Seminars have been conducted to train the participants in assertive behavior. What is this assertiveness? **Webster** defines it as a tendency, characterized by self-confidence, determination, and boldness in asserting opinions. Undoubtedly it is a needed characteristic in a competitive environment. It is also a mark of leadership. Assertiveness implies that your opinion is founded on solid truth and that you have nothing to be afraid of.

Assertiveness lifts you from being passive and submissive, when you are in the right. However, assertiveness should not be mistaken for aggressiveness. Exercising assertiveness at the right situations is, of course, desirable in interpersonal communications. It is not only what you say, but how you say it.

How to Recognize and Deal with Difficult People

Recognizing a 'difficult' person is not difficult. The immediately manifestive symptom is his or her lack of friendliness and a 'don't care' facial expression. He is not the first to offer his hand for a casual hand-shake. Many do not even respond to your polite mention of a simple "good morning".

In an office situation if he is a boss, he tends to be stiffnecked and often rude in routine dealings. He is egoistical and nurtures the notion that he is at one step higher than you in the hierarchy, and therefore his opinion is always better than yours. He would rather like you to call him by his last name. If he is a subordinate, he will just do the assigned job; he will not show inclination to be either goal-oriented or task-oriented. I don't have to indicate how to recognize difficult persons outside of the office or at home. You know them: unfriendly, non-smiling, and non-cooperative.

How to deal with them? My suggestion is that you keep your cool under all circumstances. Go by situational ethics; be assertive where you should, but be polite. Remember that the other person is the problem and not you. Since you are aiming for excellence in your interpersonal relationship, your personal code of ethics of behavior should be better than those 'difficult' people.

How to Recognize Your Friends and Hold the Friendship

Not all 'friendly' people are friends. We mentioned earlier that every person has an innate, latent element of fondness or dislike for the other person. Friendship develops between people with compatible elements. How do we know? The manifestive symptom is the feeling of happiness while being in the company of a friend. This feeling is spontaneous and can not be faked. It is the hallmark of being human. Of course, you know that you do not get this feeling from all people with whom you meet and deal. You are simply being polite with them during your interaction as one should.

Friendship is more than the feeling of joy. For the friendship to grow further interactive experiences are needed. Each experience is a building block of the friendship. The first sign of the strengthening relationship is a sense of caring for the other person. You become sensitive to the other person's feelings and respect the other's views.

The second manifestive sign of friendship is the total acceptance of the other person as he or she is, physically and mentally, as a person. Without this totality of acceptance, no true friendship is possible. Further, "a friend in need is a friend indeed." A true friend comes to your rescue when you may need help because he or she cares for you. Friendship is not for happy get-togethers only. A true friend takes the liberty to point out your mistakes and errors you are likely to commit or you have committed in your undertakings, but you are not aware of.

However strong the friendship is, you should remember that it is mutual and hangs on a thin web. It is fragile and brittle, and you should handle it with utmost care and respect. It is something that you can not take for granted.

Nurturing the friendship with occasional gifts, dinners and inquiring phone calls, and showing a readiness to be of help when needed tend to keep the friendship alive and well. A word of caution in maintaining a healthy friendship is in order: never try to take advantage of your friendship for personal, selfish gains. That is the surest way to destroy the friendship.

Remember that though people keep changing psychologically as they grow older, a good friendship built on mutual trust and respect can endure a lifetime. If there is one thing that money can not buy in this world, it is true friendship.

How to Heal Strained Relationships

It is not always that you break a relationship and forget about it. Often there is a need to mend a strained relationship for various reasons such as working in the same office, being neighbors, living in the same family, etc. If you realize that you are at fault, don't hesitate to admit it and ask to be pardoned. If the other person is at fault in your opinion, then wait for a couple of days till your anger subsides and then keep a polite distance from that person, but don't forget to say "Hi."

Often people are angry at each other for no apparent reason. In such cases, invariably, some kind of subliminal jealousy in trying to compete for the same favors is lurking in the background. Professional jealousy in offices and factories have often been found in people due to this same reason. There is no cure for this, except that by being aware of it you can at least protect yourself by accepting the poor relationship and not showing undue hostility and resentment openly.

The proverbial mother-in-law/daughter-in-law relationship has this element of subliminal jealousy in it over the territorial right on the son/husband. Close friends becoming bitter enemies over a common boy or girl friend is not uncommon. It takes courage and magnanimity to accept the loss and bow to the winning suitor.

Marriage

Between husband and wife the relationship is very different from all others. They have a personal commitment to stand by each other during good and bad days and to help each other at times of need—at least that is what they had agreed to. Marriage is an on-the-job learning experience, and a loving relationship can not be taken for granted. It has to evolve through the process of giving and taking through the ups and downs of family life. It is here that most couples hit the rocks, and they blame it on incompatibility. "Forget and forgive" is an age-old remedy and is still good for the modern times, if only they are willing to take time to forget and forgive.

Accept What You Can Not Change

I am not suggesting that there is a ready-made solution for every strained relationship. Human interrelationship is very complex and dynamic and spills far beyond the seven laws of behavior we mentioned earlier in this chapter. While you can not change the other person's attitude and behavior, you have at least some control on how you want to relate to others. Accept what you can not change, and that is the best attitude and behavior modification on your part in such situations. It is a mark of self-excellence.

Chapter **14**

Step 5—Towards Excellence In Eating and Drinking Habits

"If you reject the undesirable food and eat the desirable food in the right quantity and at the right time, there will be no disease for the body."

Thiruvalluvar
3rd century B.C. philosopher, poet, and saint of India
Author of *Thirukural*

All the stress management and the self-excellence techniques we have discussed so far will be meaningful and efficacious only when you adhere to a few basic and fundamental principles of good diet and nutrition for the body. Lack of understanding and control of the dietary principles and intake of food will seriously jeopardize your health, adding burden to the bodily ills brought about by physical and mental stress as we had seen before. The old saying that you are what you eat makes a lot of sense when you consider what happens to the food you eat and what it does to your body, and, for that matter of fact, to your mind. Step 5 aims at an understanding of the effects of the food and drink we take. This will pave the way for excellence in your eating and drinking habits.

The Nutrients in Food

Eating is an integral part of our living. Your ideas regarding what to eat, when to eat, and how much to eat constitute an important aspect of your knowledge related to food. The primary role of food is to nourish the body, and the food chosen wisely will provide all the nutrients essential for the normal functioning of the body.

However, if food is not chosen wisely, there will be a deficiency of one or more of the essential nutrients needed for the body on one hand, and the possible accumulation of cholesterol and saturated fat on the other, leading to problems of the cardiovascular system and overweight.

The nutrients in the food you take serve the following functions: to supply energy to the body as a whole, to promote the growth and repair of body tissues and to regulate body processes. The nutrients that carry out these functions are grouped into five main categories, namely carbohydrate, fat, protein, minerals, and vitamins. Water, the single most important component of the food, acts as the solvent for the nutrients and transports them to all parts of the body. It is significant to note that water constitutes 60 percent of all the body weight.

Effect of Stress on Eating

Eating is a basic biological need expressed by the feelings of hunger. Neurophysiologists consider that the hypothalamus of the brain, the regulatory center for both the sympathetic and parasympathetic divisions of the autonomic nervous system, alerts us when we need food and water through the impulses of hunger and thirst, and also informs us when they are satisfied.

However, in a person under stress the normal signals of hunger and thirst are influenced by the stress hormones in the blood stream, and as a result he or she does not respond to those signals as one would under stress-free circumstances. Some respond by eating more than they need to, and some eating less. If the unresolved stress persists over a long period of time, the person may end up with a changed eating habit and pattern as a subliminal defense against the unpleasant consequences of the stress. This may lead him or her to a state of malnutrition through either overeating or undereating. You may recall from our earlier discussions that stress plays a decisive role in increasing the cholesterol level of the blood which, over a long period of time, tends to get deposited on the walls of the blood vessels, thus directly contributing to the hardening of the arteries, known as atherosclerosis.

Two Deadly Enemies: Excess Cholesterol And Saturated Triglyceride

Cholesterol

Cholesterol, a fat-related substance present in the blood, the brain and other tissues throughout the body and in many foods we eat, is essential to life. The outer membrane of the body's various cells, particularly in the fatty sheath that insulates the nerves contains cholesterol as its principal building block. Chemically it is a sterol, a complex secondary alcohol, related to Vitamin D, the sex hormones, and hormones of the adrenal cortex. It is soluble in fat, though highly insoluble in water. See Table 2 for cholesterol content of some of the most common foods.

The body's needs for cholesterol are met with by its own manufacturing process, mainly in the liver. The liver continuously produces a bitter, greenish-yellow fluid called bile which contains bile salts, cholesterol, and other chemical substances. Bile is stored in the gall bladder. Whenever fat in the food we eat leaves the stomach and enters the small intestine, it stimulates the flow of bile from both the liver and the gall bladder. The bile enters the small intestine through a small tube, the common bile duct, and helps in the digestion and absorption of fats. The fat broken down by the bile fluid of the liver is firmly packaged in a very soluble high density lipoprotein coating with the right amount and type of cholesterol needed by the body's various cells. In this form the liver-made cholesterol is carried in the blood stream and is readily absorbed by the body's cells during the course of the blood circulation.

However, beside the liver-made cholesterol, the blood serum is loaded with a poorly-synthesized cholesterol package from the intestine, containing fatty substances, known as tryglycerides, coated with very low density lipoproteins. These packages leave the intestinal cells and reach the general blood circulation through the ducts of the lymphatic system. Once these packages are delivered to the body's various tissue cells, lipoprotein enzymes are released which separate triglycerides from the carrier proteins. In this process not all tryglycerides are absorbed by the body's cells. The unabsorbed packages become a cholesterol-rich fatty substance floating in the blood serum,

Food	Amount	Cholesterol (mg)
Milk, skim, fluid or reconstituted dry	1 cup	5
Cottage cheese, uncreamed	½ cup	7
Lard	1 tablespoon	12
Cream, light table	1 fl. oz.	20
Cottage cheese, creamed	½ cup	24
Cream, half and half	¼ cup	26
Ice cream, regular, approximately 10% fat	½ cup	27
Cheese, cheddar	1 oz.	28
Milk, whole	1 cup	34
Butter	1 tablespoon	35
Oysters, salmon	3 oz. cooked	40
Clams, halibut, tuna	3 oz. cooked	55
Chicken, turkey, light meat	3 oz. cooked	67
Beef, pork, lobster, chicken, turkey—dark meat	3 oz. cooked	75
Lamb, veal, crab	3 oz. cooked	85
Shrimp	3 oz. cooked	130
Heart, beef	3 oz. cooked	230
Egg	1 yolk or 1 egg	250
Liver, beef, calf, hog, lamb	3 oz. cooked	370
Kidney	3 oz. cooked	680
Brains	3 oz. raw	More than 1700

From Fats in food and diet, Agricultural Information Bulletin No. 361, 1974, Washington, D.C., U.S Department of Agriculture.

Table 2. Cholesterol content of selected foods.

increasing the cholesterol and triglyceride level of the blood. It has been found in many studies that heart disease occurred most often in persons who had a high blood cholesterol level coupled with a high blood triglyceride level.

Triglycerides appear in the blood after a meal high in saturated fat. Medical science has many recorded instances of people dying of a heart attack following a heavy meal rich in animal fat. The triglyceride released from the intestine cells have been known to be the culprit in forming blood clots in the already cholesterol-rich blood serum and blocking the coronary arteries.

Fat Differences

Like carbohydrates, fat is composed of the three elements carbon, hydrogen, and oxygen. However, it differs from carbohydrate in that the ratio of oxygen to carbon and hydrogen is much lower such as 1:2 in simple carbohydrates, whereas it can be as high as 1:30 in simple fats. It is this lower amount of oxygen in relation to the other two elements accounts for the fact that fat is a more concentrated form of energy than is carbohydrate.

Dietary fats are composed of two major biochemical components—glycerol and fatty acids. Whereas the glycerol portion is common to practically all dietary fats, the fatty acid portion varies from one fat to another. Then again, the nature of the chemical bond that exists between the carbon and hydrogen atoms in the fatty acid divides it into two categories—saturated fatty acid and unsaturated fatty acid. In a saturated fatty acid, 2 hydrogen atoms, the maximum possible, are attached to each carbon atom other than the first and the last in the chain. In contrast, unsaturated fatty acids have fewer than the maximum number of hydrogen atoms attached to the carbon chain.

Triglyceride

A fat that has one molecule of fatty acid attached to a glycerol molecule is called monoglyceride. Diglyceride has two fatty acids attached to the glycerol, whereas triglyceride has three. The most common fats are triglycerides, accounting for about 95 percent of fat in our food. See Figure 31.

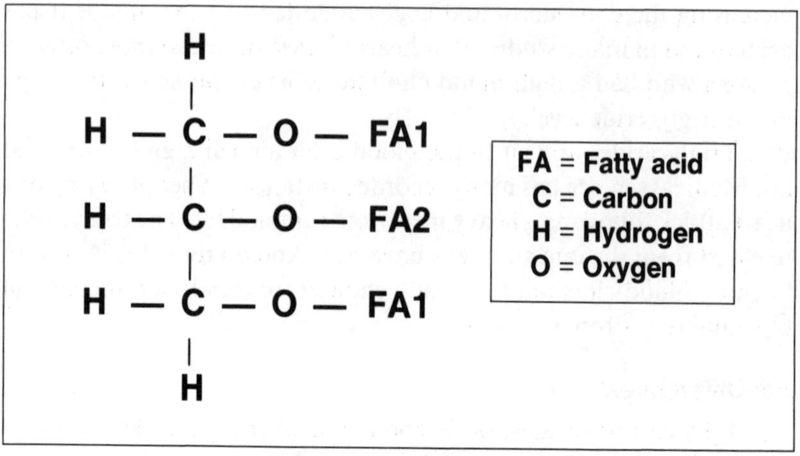

```
        H
        |
H  —  C  —  O  —  FA1
        |
H  —  C  —  O  —  FA2
        |
H  —  C  —  O  —  FA1
        |
        H
```

FA = Fatty acid
C = Carbon
H = Hydrogen
O = Oxygen

Figure 31. Triglycerides

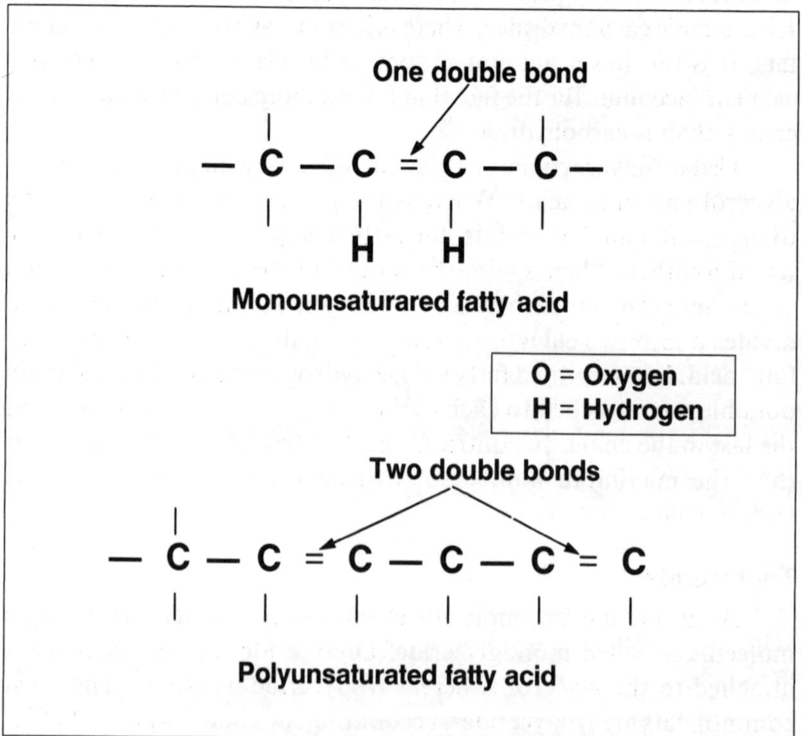

One double bond

```
    |        |
—  C  —  C  =  C  —  C  —
    |        |     |     |
             H     H
```

Monounsaturared fatty acid

O = Oxygen
H = Hydrogen

Two double bonds

```
    |
—  C  —  C  =  C  —  C  —  C  =  C
    |    |     |     |     |     |
```

Polyunsaturated fatty acid

Figure 32. Unsaturated Fatty Acids

From the health point of view, unsaturated dietary fats are preferable over the saturated ones. Many medical studies investigating coronary problems have now confirmed the existence of the link between premature heart attack and a diet rich in cholesterol and saturated fat.

Saturated Fats ("Undesirable" Fats)

Fats with saturated fatty acids tend to be solid at room temperature and will have a high melting point. These include: fatty meats like beef, veal, lamb and pork; luncheon meats; butter; whole milk; cheese; eggs; lard; shellfish; chocolate; thick gravies; cream; coconut; desserts and pastries made with animal fat or butter.

Unsaturated Fats ("Desirable" Fats)

Unsaturated fatty acids, having fewer than the maximum number of hydrogen atoms attached to the carbon chain produce a fat that is liquid at room temperature with a low melting point. When one hydrogen atom is missing from each 2 adjacent carbons, the 2 carbons form an additional chemical bond, known as a double bond, in the carbon chain to compensate for the loss of hydrogen atoms. See Figure 32. Fatty acids having one double bond only in their molecular structure are called as monounsaturated fatty acids. Poultry and most nuts are rich sources for the monounsaturated fat.

In some fatty acids double bonds appear in 2 or more places in the molecular structure, and these are known as polyunsaturated fatty acids. Fish, walnuts and most vegetable oils like corn oil, safflower oil, peanut oil, cottonseed oil and soybean oil are rich in polyunsaturated fats.

P/S Ratio in Food Items

You might have noticed in the commercial advertising and food labels a P/S ratio for the food item. A P/S ratio refers to the proportion of unsaturated to saturated fatty acids in the fat contained in the food. The higher the P/S ratio, the more unsaturated fatty acids are present in the fat and the more likely it is to be liquid. The higher the P/S ratio, the better it is from low-cholesterol point of view.

In general, animal fats are high in saturated fatty acids, whereas vegetable fats are low in them. Chicken fat and fish are exceptions to this and they have a high P/S ratio. Coconut oil is another exception. It has a low P/S ratio but is liquid at room temperature. This low ratio is due to the large proportion of short-chain fatty acids which are highly saturated.

It is important to note here that from a low-cholesterol point of view, preference must be given to chicken and fish over other meats, and vegetable seed oils must be preferred over coconut oil and artificially-hydrogenated oils.

Low-Cholesterol, Low-Fat Diet

In the light of the above discussion, you will note that it makes sense to limit the amount of fat and cholesterol in the diet in any stress management program. **Helen Guthrie,** in her book, *Introductory Nutrition,* recommends the following:

(1) the amount of fat in the diet must be reduced to 35 percent of total caloric intake;

(2) the amount of dietary cholesterol must be restricted to less than 300 milligram;

(3) saturated fat must be limited to 15 percent of total caloric intake;

(4) wherever possible substitute polyunsaturated fat for polysaturated fat in the diet;

(5) caloric intake must be adjusted to maintain desirable body weight.

Low Salt Diet

It has been known long to the medical profession that excess salt in the diet contributes to high blood pressure. A study of the diet habits of Eskimos found that they take very little salt in their diet, and it also found that high blood pressure and stroke are very rare among them. Another study found that the Japanese, who are large salt consumers, have a high incidence of both.

It is important in a stress management program to realize that high salt intake can intensify an existing tendency toward hypertension while a low-salt diet can help keep it under control. Since the relationship between stress and high blood pressure has been well established, it makes sense for a stressed person to adhere to a low-salt diet.

EATING AND DRINKING HABITS

Table salt, as the chemical sodium chloride is commonly known, contains sodium, an essential mineral required by the body. While present in proper amount, it helps to maintain the body's acid-base balance, and water balance, besides contributing to catalytic action of many of the body's enzymes. However, when the sodium intake exceeds the ability of the kidneys to excrete it, the level of sodium in the blood and the intercellular fluid of the body's tissues increases, leading to an increase in the osmotic pressure of the body fluids. The body's cells respond by losing their fluids to the sodium-concentrated intercellular fluid in an attempt to dilute it. This causes an increase in the volume of blood and intercellular fluid. It is this increase in the blood that results in elevated blood pressure.

Conversely, if the levels of sodium fall, there is a contraction of blood volume, a drop in blood pressure, a decrease in intercellular fluid, and fluid balance is restored to the cells.

Since the body's sodium need is easily satisfied from the intake of a balanced diet, throwing extra salt into the food constitutes a health hazard for a person who is already tensed up under stress and whose blood pressure is high.

Weight Control

Further, it is essential in stress management and in striving for self-excellence to maintain body weight within the limits compatible with maximum level of health, or to adjust body weight to conform to the established standards. Weight accumulates only when energy intake exceeds energy expenditure, and the possibility of this occurring is influenced by psychological, physiological, social, cultural and genetic factors. Psychologists have found that stressed persons with distorted self-image problems have a tendency to overeat. Anxiety and frustration have been known to make people seek solace in food, the consumption of which represents a pleasurable pastime. However, it may result in an undesirable gain in body weight, which medical science has long since recognized as a health hazard.

Weight Table

The desirable range of body weight for men and women, recommended by the **American Medical Association,** is given in Table 3. Ideally, your weight should remain constant after the age of 25.

Desirable Weights for Men, Ages Twenty-Five and Over

Height (with shoes, 1-in. heels)		Weights in Pounds According to Frame (as ordinarily dressed)		
Feet	Inches	Small Frame	Medium Frame	Large Frame
5	2	112-120	118-129	126-141
5	3	115-123	121-133	129-144
5	4	118-126	124-136	132-148
5	5	121-129	127-139	135-152
5	6	124-133	130-143	138-156
5	7	128-137	134-147	142-161
5	8	132-141	138-152	147-166
5	9	136-145	142-156	151-170
5	10	140-150	146-160	155-174
5	11	144-154	150-165	159-179
6	0	148-158	154-170	164-184
6	1	152-162	158-175	168-189
6	2	156-167	162-180	173-194
6	3	160-171	167-185	178-199
6	4	164-175	172-190	182-204

Source: Metropolitan Life Insurance Company. Derived previously from data of the Build and Blood Pressure Study, 1959, Society of Actuaries.

Desirable Weights for Women, Ages Twenty-Five and Over

Height (with shoes, 2-in. heels)		Weights in Pounds According to Frame (as ordinarily dressed)		
Feet	Inches	Small Frame	Medium Frame	Large Frame
4	10	92-98	96-107	104-119
4	11	94-101	98-110	106-122
5	0	96-104	101-113	109-125
5	1	99-107	104-116	112-128
5	2	102-110	107-119	115-131
5	3	105-113	110-122	118-134
5	4	108-116	113-126	121-138
5	5	111-119	116-130	125-142
5	6	114-123	120-135	129-146
5	7	118-127	124-139	133-150
5	8	122-131	128-143	137-154
5	9	126-135	132-147	141-158
5	10	130-140	136-151	145-163
5	11	134-144	140-155	149-168
6	4	138-148	144-159	153-173

Source: Metropolitan Life Insurance Company. Derived previously from data of the Build and Blood Pressure Study, 1959, Society of Actuaries.

Table 3. Desirable body weight.

Balanced Diet

Besides paying attention to weight control, it is essential that you should eat a balanced diet. A balanced diet contains adequate quantities of proteins, carbohydrates and fats—all of which provide energy, and vitamins, minerals and fibers for effective body functioning. Thus a balanced diet gives you all the nutrients and energy you need, but no more. Following are some pointers to help you maintain a balanced diet, recommended by the American Medical Association.

1. Do not eat meat more than once a day. Choose fish and poultry in place of red meat, sausages and processed meat. Fish and poultry are less fattening and low in cholesterol.
2. Baking or broiling food is better than frying it. If you have to fry, use polyunsaturated oils (such as corn oil) rather than butter, lard or saturated margarines.
3. Cut down on salt and other sodium containing substances in your diet such as meat tenderizers (monosodium glutamate or MSG).
4. Get your daily requirement of fiber by eating plenty of leafy vegetables and fruit. Eating them raw or lightly cooked preserves the essential vitamins, which are otherwise destroyed by prolonged cooking. Another good source of fiber is potato skins.
5. Eat no more than a total of four eggs a week. Though eggs are low in saturated fat, they have a very high cholesterol content.
6. For dessert or a snack choose fresh fruit rather than cakes, cookies or puddings.

Remember that the golden rule in diet is "moderation." Too much of anything, whether it is the number of calories you consume or a certain kind of food, is unwise. Finally, in addition to choosing a balanced and adequate meal, it is equally important to sit down and relax at meal time and enjoy what you eat.

Stress, Alcohol and Relaxation

Associating alcohol with a relaxed evening is a cherished notion for many people. A drink or two may help to create an aura of relaxation, leaving cares and worries forgotten temporarily, and may encourage sociability. At the end of a stressful workday an unhurried drink can ameliorate some of the tensions of the day, opening the way for a relaxed dinner and relaxed evening. However, you must remember that alcohol is a drug, and any drug consumed in excess, or at the wrong time can be harmful.

Some people under stressful situations turn to alcohol, believing that they can manage their problems better after a drink or two. There is nothing unhealthy about taking one or even two average strength drinks of hard liquor—about two ounces per day. Taken this way, alcohol can serve as a tranquilizer or relaxant and as an improver of appetite.

The Effects of Alcohol

One major reason why many people enjoy moderate drinking is the relaxing effect induced by the alcohol due to gradual dulling of the reactions of the brain and the nervous system. Even in small quantities, alcohol is not a stimulant, as many erroneously believe.

Alcohol begins to be absorbed into the blood stream as soon as it enters the stomach and begins to circulate within a couple of minutes. It is specially fast acting when taken on an empty stomach. While it is possible to become drunk fairly quickly, sobering up takes much longer.

The blood carries the alcohol to the liver, then to the heart, the lungs, and the brain where it usually has its most important effects. In fact, alcohol acts as a depressant; that is, it slows down the activity and impairs the efficiency of the central nervous system. It is possible that the drinker feels stimulated from having had a drink. This is due to the fact that alcohol dulls or depresses the higher brain centers, casting off the person's anxieties and inhibitions and making him feel happy and carefree.

Dangers of Alcohol

However, the world of alcohol is very deceptive, and it drags in many a so-called "social drinker" into a state of dependence on alcohol slowly without his or her being aware of it. What happens is that the cells of the body accommodate the presence of alcohol and their tolerance level increases. Due to this increased tolerance the drinker has to take an increased quantity of alcohol to provide the same effect as before, trying to relax himself—unaware of the continuously increasing alcohol content in his blood circulation.

Though medical science has not fully understood the mechanism of this alcohol-dependence at the cellular level, it appears that the cells of the body may shift their metabolism. For their nourishment the cells, of course, depend upon the circulating blood. As they are exposed to the alcohol in the blood, they develop the tendency to accommodate to the presence of the alcohol. As a result, they have become as dependent upon alcohol being there as they once were upon it not being there. At this point, it is difficult for the "social drinker" to stop drinking. He has become addicted to alcohol. If the addict's alcohol supply is cut off suddenly, he reacts with distressing symptoms, including violent tremors, nausea and headaches.

Alcohol dulls the cerebral cortex, an area of the brain that is associated with judgment, motor coordination and self-control. As muscular control decreases reaction time becomes greater. For example, a driver, who has had several drinks is unable to stop or swerve in an emergency as quickly as he would normally when sober.

Most of the alcohol in the body is handled by the liver, and as such most damage is done to this organ. Cirrhosis of the liver is the most common ailment of the chronic alcoholics. Excessive drinking affects the nervous system, producing painful nerve inflammation as well as impairing memory and intellectual powers. It also affects the sex impulse adversely. Besides, drinking affects not only the victim but spouse and children as well, often leading to traumatic experiences and psychosomatic illnesses among the latter.

For these obvious reasons the quest for genuine relaxation in a stress management program does not consider alcohol as a means because of the danger of the aspirant being led to alcoholism with all its attendant undesirable effects on the body and mind.

Intelligent Drinking

If you consider yourself a disciplined person and if you know when to stop as far as alcoholic beverages are concerned, then you may be able to enjoy the relaxation through alcohol by adhering to a few simple rules of intelligent drinking. It is primarily a matter of timing as well as moderation. The time to drink is at the end of a taxing work day, not at lunch and not after dinner. American Medical Association suggests the following five rules:

1. **Set Reasonable Limits for Yourself**
   Do not exceed a predecided number of drinks on a given occasion, and stick to your decision. No more than two beers or two cocktails a day is a reasonable limit.

2. **Learn to Say No**
   When you have reached the sensible limit you have set for yourself, politely but firmly refuse to exceed it, no matter who puts pressure on you.

3. **Drink Slowly**
   Do not gulp down a drink. Choose your drinks wisely for their flavor, not their "kick," and enjoy the taste of each sip.

4. **Dilute Your Drinks**
   If you prefer cocktails to beer, try to have long drinks. Instead of drinking your gin or whisky straight, drink it diluted with a mixer such as tonic, water or soda water, in a tall glass.

5. **Do Not Drink on Your Own**
   Make it a point to confine your drinking only to social gatherings, and never drink alone. The urge to relax yourself at the end of a hard day with an alcoholic beverage can be as well satisfied with a cup of coffee or a soft drink over a television program or with a good book to read.

Chapter 15

Drugs and Smoking/ Their Effects On the Body

"The mortal body is a temple of nine gates where the immortal Self resides. The wise shall desist from willful pollution and destruction of the temple premises."

3000 year-old Upanishadhic wisdom

In the quest for relaxation and freedom from their cares and pressures of the real world they live in, many people turn to drugs and smoking. Do these really help in alleviating the anxieties of the individual and minimize the ill-effects of stress? What is their place in a program of stress management? In this chapter we shall explore the effects of the use of drugs and smoking on the body and mind of the relaxation seeker.

Stress, Drugs, and Relaxation

The notion that certain drugs induce relaxation and reduce stress is valid only for the medically prescribed sedatives used under the direction of a physician for specific ailments. When used in normal, prescribed doses sedatives, such as barbiturates, mildly depress nerve activity, slow the heart rate and breathing, and lower blood pressure—the same type of physiological effects observed in many relaxation techniques. The comparison stops there; because in the use of any relaxation method, the person retains complete control of his senses and cognition processes. But, this is not the case with a person using a drug.

Besides, sedatives produce tolerance, requiring increasingly greater doses to achieve the same effects. Worst yet is that they produce physical dependence. Their sudden withdrawal can lead to physical discomforts like nausea, delirium, and convulsions.

Barbiturates as sedatives are well known. Even in small doses they may slow the motor reaction and distort the vision. It has been observed that barbiturates are among the major causes of automobile accidents on the roads. Taken together, alcohol and barbiturates form a dangerous combination as the two substances have a synergistic effect in which each greatly increases the effects of the other.

Narcotic drugs including opium, heroin, morphine and codeine are brain and nervous system depressants. They reduce hunger, thirst, and sex drive as well as feelings of pain. Use of heroin is widespread by addicts. It produces an apparent relief from worry as a first reaction but then is followed by a state of inactivity of the brain, bordering on semi-consciousness. All narcotic drugs have a tendency to produce tolerance and physical dependence leading to addiction.

Hallucinating drugs like LSD and stimulant drugs such as amphetamines also act on the nervous system but increase the heart rate and blood pressure, besides producing a host of undesirable physiological changes, which are the opposites of physical and mental relaxation. These are the very effects which a person seeking genuine relaxation is trying to get away from.

Dangers of Drug Addiction

Since many a stressed person is likely to turn to drugs hoping to find some relief however temporary it may be, I would like to point out the inherent dangers of drug addiction. Anyone who is addicted to a hard drug must take it in gradually increasing doses to maintain the pleasurable effects of the drug and to keep from breaking down physically and mentally due to the building up of tolerance to the drug. If the addict's need for the drug is not satisfied, unpleasant physical and psychological effects called withdrawal symptoms will result. In some cases these symptoms can be harmful, or even fatal, and hence the withdrawal from the drug should be medically supervised.

In general, any addiction is likely to cause a gradual deterioration of the addict's standards of work, personal relationships, or both. Very often, the behavior of addicts is erratic and their moods may be changeable, with periods of restlessness and irritability alternating with extreme drowsiness. Taken habitually hard drugs violently upset the body's chemical balance. In extreme cases it can cause serious physical or mental illness, even death.

Since having the body and mind under our complete control is seriously impaired by all drugs, the question of using any of them in a stress management program does not arise at all. A serious aspirant of genuine relaxation will do well to keep away from them.

Stress, Smoking, and Relaxation

The commercial advertisements for cigarettes in the newspapers, magazines, bill-boards, and elsewhere would have us believe that cigarette smoking is associated with a sense of pleasant relaxation. It is not unusual to see many office workers, executives and others to light up one cigarette after another during the course of their busy work and stressful situations. It is claimed in their favor that they use cigarettes to reduce uncomfortable feelings—anxiety, tension, boredom, anger, fear, etc.,—in the same way others turn to chemical tranquilizers.

But, does cigarette smoking really induce relaxation in a person under stress? Unfortunately, no! Let us take an objective look at what happens during smoking and how it affects the physiological system. As the cigarette is lit, the smoker invariably inhales the smoke which goes to the lungs, and his pulse count goes up anywhere from 5 to 15 beats, indicating an increase in his blood pressure. In fact, the cigarette, instead of bringing relaxation, has brought additional stress to the heart—although the smoker may have the psychological impression that it has helped him or her to relax! How did this happen?

The tobacco smoke, whether it is from cigarettes, cigars, or pipes, contains many different substances, among them the three dangerous chemicals: tar, nicotine and carbon monoxide. See Figure 33. The nicotine, absorbed directly from the lungs filled with the smoke or from the mucous membrane of the mouth, excites the sympathetic nervous centers in the brain. As a result, the oxygen-wasting hormones adrenaline and noradrenaline are injected into the blood stream. In order to make up for the oxygen deficiency, the heart works faster and harder, as seen from the increased heart-beat rate and blood pressure.

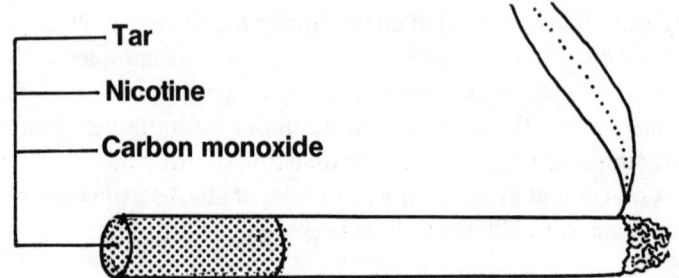

Figure 33. The 3 Chemicals of Cigarette Smoke.

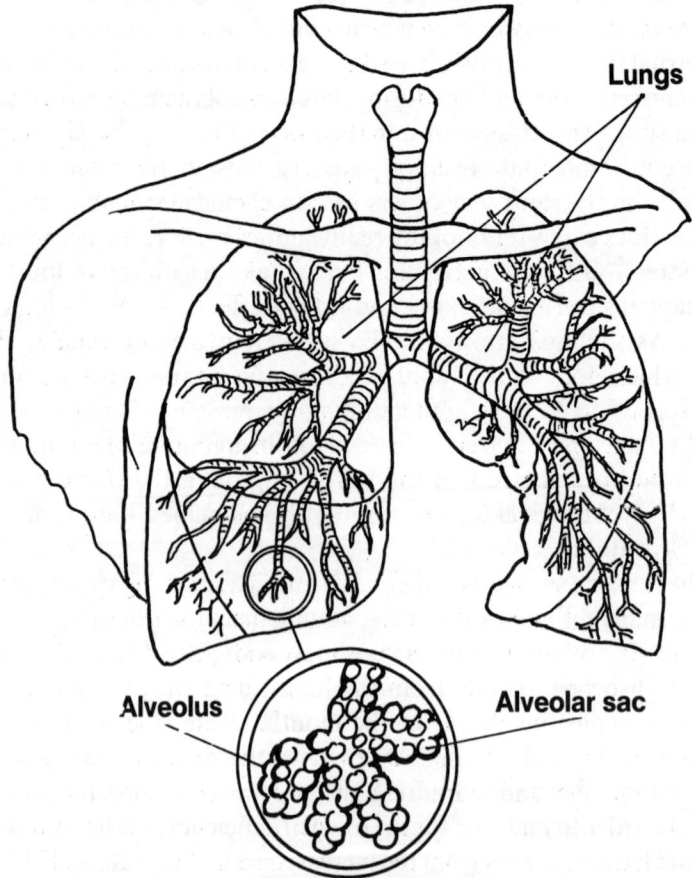

Figure 34. Airsac of lungs.

DRUGS AND SMOKING

Carbon monoxide in the tobacco smoke combines with hemoglobin, the oxygen-carrying substance in red blood cells. Studies have shown that as much as 6 percent of the hemoglobin in the blood of an average smoker is taken up and inactivated by carbon monoxide. Thus, taking the place of oxygen, carbon monoxide leads to shortness of breath on exertion.

Tar is a mixture of several substances in the smoke, and it condenses into a sticky substance in the air sacs of the lungs. The lungs contain millions of air sacs, known as alveoli. These air sacs receive carbon dioxide from the blood and exchange it for the oxygen from the air breathed into the lungs. The tar sticks to the inner surface of the air sacs, interfering with the vital oxygen-carbon dioxide exchange of the breathing process. See Figure 34. As a result, the blood tends to become overloaded with carbon dioxide. Also, tar being an irritant produces mucus in the walls of the air sacs which plugs up the small air tubes leading to the airsacs. Thus, the smoke in the tobacco paves the way for cough, bronchitis, and emphysema and also increases the risk of lung cancer.

Stimulant and Depressant

Because of the nicotine, cigarette smoking produces an immediate feeling of stimulation by activating the nervous system and other glands, producing release of some sugar from the liver. As a result, the smoker feels a sense of exhilaration and a "kick." With smoking the heart rate increases and the blood pressure rises. Scientists believe that the nicotine in the blood tends to constrict the smaller arteries, reducing blood flow and lowering skin temperature. However, as the nicotine level in the blood decreases, the nervous system becomes depressed and the smoker feels a sense of fatigue. To relieve the fatigue he lights up another cigarette!

Smoking and Heart Problems

Many studies have shown that smoking speeds the clotting of blood, which increases risk of clot formation in the arteries of the heart. Also, smoking places additional pressure on the heart, forcing it to pump more blood more rapidly because the carbon monoxide from smoke redues the oxygen-carrying capacity of the blood and impairs the elasticity and gas-exchange capacity of the lungs. Recent studies have clearly confirmed that cigarette smoking is among the most important risk factors in the occurrence of heart attack.

Dangers of Smoking: The Surgeon General's Warning

Viewed from any angle the evidences point out that cigarette smoking contributes only negatively to the physical and psychological well being of the smoker. Reaching for a cigarette under stressful situations does more harm than any good and tends to start the vicious cycle of cigarette addiction, with all the attendent trauma of any drug addiction. In a stress management program it is worthwhile paying attention to the warning of the United States Surgeon General that cigarette smoking is dangerous to your health. A wise person does not go against sensible warnings based on medically verified facts.

EPILOG

Create Your Own Plans and Goals

Now that you have read the blueprint for self-excellence and have learned about its place in preventive stress management and creative living, it is up to you to work out your own integrated master plan for your life. No matter what your goals are, you can achieve them through commitment, hard work, and discipline, if the goals are realistic and in line with your uniqueness characteristic.

Self-excellence is at the core of every human being. It is like **Michelangelo's** sculpture. A visitor asked him how he was able to make such a beautiful figure out of a shapeless, massive rock. **Michelangelo** replied that he did not make it; it was already there. All he did was to chip away the excess debris!

Remember that homeostasis of the body, equanimity of the mind, and creativity of the intellect are the triple signs of self-excellence. By a judicious adaptation of the 5-steps suiting your life style and matching your uniqueness characteristic, you should be able to manage most of your stressors and even prevent them in many situations. In this adaptation lies the essence of a creative living.

The following is a set of guide lines for planning your own goal-oriented life of self-excellence with preventive stress management techniques.

1. Take time to contemplate the state of your life, personal and professional, and make an objective evaluation. Note the problematic areas which are stressful, and note the things that you always wanted to do, but did not or could not.

2. Take additional time to analyze yourself as a person, your likes and dislikes, and your past responses to stressful situations. Discover your weaknesses and strengths in the mental plane. In finding your uniqueness characteristic, you will be happy and comfortable with yourself in certain types of activities which help you easily lose yourself. You may have more than one of them. This characteristic is the key for your creative living.

3. Set goals for yourself for personal fulfillment, professional advancement, and family commitments. Integrate these goals with those of your spouse at home, and those of your source of employment so that no conflicts are encountered. When your goals are in tune with your uniqueness characteristic, you will have the greatest satisfaction and you will be able to develop yourself to the fullness of your potentials.

4. "Accept and adapt" is the starting point. Accept yourself as you are and start building a new planned life with necessary attitude and behavior modifications through the principles of self-excellence.

5. Spend a minimum of 20 minutes a day for physical fitness and maintaining a desirable cardiovascular endurance level recommended by your doctor. Choose the type of exercises that you like and that suits your living pattern. Keep the exercise program on a fixed routine, at least 5 days a week. Incidentally, this provides relief and relaxation for the physiological stress built-up during the day.

6. Spend another 20 minutes a day as a routine for complete withdrawal from your activities and retire to a quiet place for exploration of your inner-self. Bring yourself to the alpha state of relaxation and contemplate on your inner-personality. Learn to use the technique of visualization to build a positive self-image and emotion management.

7. Spend yet another 20 minutes every day for psychophysical relaxation and creativity. Use this time for the development of your creative potential and learning new skills. This provides opportunity for you for self-expression and self-fulfillment along with the achievement of new goals.
8. Learn the principles of effective interpersonal relationship and make use of it during the course of daily living. Be always polite and self-assured. Try to see the other person's point of view in any situation before responding to him or her in difficult situations. Excellence in interpersonal communication is preventive and therapeutic, as far as stress management is concerned. Also, it wins you many friends and influences other people.
9. Build the habit of paying attention to what you eat and drink. "Every meal a sensible meal, every drink a sensible drink" should be your motto. Your aim should be to have a balanced diet with all the proper nutrients, from protein, to vitamins, minerals, fats and carbohydrates. Avoid high cholesterol and high saturated fat products such as red meat and pork and go for poultry, fish, and vegetables. Avoid alcoholic beverages altogether if you can; otherwise, be moderate and stick with the principles of intelligent drinking.
10. Avoid drugs of any kind except under medical supervision. As far as smoking is concerned, heed to the Surgeon General's warning that smoking is hazardous to your health.
11. Plan for periodic family vacations as a part of your goal-oriented living. Vacations break the monotony of routine living and bring rest and relaxation from the pressures of the profession. They provide the opportunity to explore the world around you in all its man-made and nature-made splendors.
12. Join a community service club in your area or a church group and take part in activities to extend a helping hand to needy people—local, national or international. Reaching out to help others is a sign of human sensitivity and also a mark of self-excellence.

Self-excellence is not a static process. It is continuous and dynamic. **It is a way of life.** Once it becomes *your* way of life, your life takes a different turn—for the better. Your perception of the world becomes different; it is no longer a place to compete and push ahead, but it is a place to live in unison with the cosmic forces that brought you here and to enjoy the fruits of your own endeavors in a coordinated life plan to which you have given your best. It is a place where you bloom to your full potentials because you are a cosmic flower. That is the message of the philosophy of self-excellence.

References

1. American Medical Association. *Family Medical Guide*. Random House, New York, 1982.
2. Barney, V. S., Hirst, C. C., and Jensen, C. R. *Conditioning Exercises*. The Mosby Co., 1969.
3. Benson, H. *The Relaxation Response*. Avon Publishers, New York, 1974.
4. Buscaglia, L. *Loving Each Other*. Slack Inc., Thorofare, NJ, 1984.
5. Cade, C. M. and Coxhead, N. *The Awakened Mind*. Delacarte Press, 1979.
6. Campbell, G. *The Joy of Jumping*. Richard Marek Publishers, New York, 1978.
7. Carnegie, Dale. *How to Stop Worrying and Start Living*. Simon and Schuster, New York, 1948.
8. Carnegie, Dale. *How to Win Friends and Influence People*. Simon and Schuster, New York, 1936.
9. Carruthers, M. *The Western Way of Death*. Pantheon Books, 1974.
10. Charlesworth, E. A. and Nathan, R. G. *Stress Management*. Athenium, New York, 1985.
11. Cooper, K. H. *Aerobics*. M. Evans and Co., New York, 1968.
12. Cooper, K. H. *New Aerobics*. M. Evans and Co., New York, 1970.
13. Cooper, Mildred. and Cooper, K. H. *Aerobics for Women*. M. Evans and Co. Inc., 1972
14. DeCoursey, R. M. *The Human Organism*. McGraw Hill Book Co., 1974.
15. Fink, D. H. *Release from Nervous Tension*. Pocket Books, Inc., New York, 1966.
16. Fredenburgh, F. A. *Exploring Human Behavior*. James E. Freel & Associates, Cupertino, CA., 1973.
17. Friedman, M. and Rosenman, R. H. *Type A Behavior and Your Heart*. Alfred Knopf, New York, 1974.

18. Guthrie, H. A. *Introductory Nutrition.* The C. V. Mosby Co., 1979.
19. Hittleman, R. L. *Yoga: The 8 Steps to Health and Peace.* Deerfield Communications, New York, 1975.
20. Hockey, R. V. *Physical Fitness.* The C. V. Mosby Co., 1973.
21. Hughes, C. L. *Goal Setting.* AMACOM, New York, 1965.
22. Langley, L. L. *Homeostasis.* Reinhold Publishing Co., 1965.
23. Levinson, H. *Executive Stress.* Harper Row Publishers, New York, 1970.
24. Maltz, Maxwell. *Psychocybernetics.* Simon & Schuster, Inc., 1960.
25. McKain, R. J. *How to Get to the Top and Stay There.* AMACOM, New York, 1981.
26. Miller, B. F. and Galton, L. *The Family Book of Preventive Medicine.* Weathervane Books, New York, 1971.
27. Mitchell, C. *The Perfect Exercise.* Simon & Schuster, New York, 1976.
28. Morgan, C. T. *Physiological Psychology.* McGraw Hill Book Co., New York, 1965.
29. Needleman, J. *A Sense of the Cosmos.* Doubleday & Co., Inc., New York, 1975.
30. Pelletier, K. R. *Mind As Healer Mind As Slayer.* Delacarte Press, 1977.
31. Sanzotta, D. *The Manager's Guide to Interpersonal Relations.* AMACOM, New York, 1979.
32. Selye, Hans. *The Stress of Life.* McGraw Hill Co. Inc., 1956.
33. Taylor, G. R. *The Natural History of the Mind.* E. P. Dutton & Co., New York, 1979.
34. Vishnudevananda, Swami. *The Complete Illustrated Book of Yoga.* Bell Publishing Co., New York, 1959.
35. Zimbardo, P. G. *Psychology and Life.* Scott, Foresman and Co., Glenview, IL., 1979.
36. *The Upanishads.* Translations from the Sanskrit. Penguin Books, Baltimore, MD., 1965.

37. *Bhagavad Gita* of Veda Vyasa. Commentary by Swami Chidbhavananda. Tapovanam Publishing House, Trichy, India, 1965.
38. *Thirukural* of Thiruvalluvar. Commentary by Parimelalagar. Saiva Siddhanta Publishing Society, Tinnevelly, India, (in Tamil), 1956.

Glossary

ADRENAL GLANDS—A pair of endocrine glands, from one to two inches in length, located at the top of the kidneys—They secrete a number of hormones, including adrenaline and cortisone, which influence many processes in the body.

ADRENALINE—A hormone that is produced by the adrenal glands—When the body is under stress, the glands increase their secretion of adrenaline and pour it into the blood, which carries it to every part of the body. The hormone speeds up the beating of the heart. It also causes an increase in blood pressure and enables the muscles to work faster and longer. It is now known medically as epinephrine.

AEROBIC EXERCISE—Any exercise program in which sufficient oxygen is supplied to the working muscles to produce the necessary energy for the performance of the exercise—Aerobic exercises are those that usually can be carried out for at least 10 minutes and during the performance of which no true oxygen debt is incurred.

ALPHA—The range of electrical activity of the brain, known as brain waves, varying from 8 to 13 times per second.

ALPHA STATE OF RELAXATION—The unstressed and relaxed waking state of a person—The brain wave frequency during this state is predominantly in the alpha range, 8 to 13 hertz. It is the most desirable waking state since the mind's cognitive and creative potentials are at their highest.

ALTERED STATE OF CONSCIOUSNESS (ASC)—A mental state in which the individual clearly feels a qualitative shift in his pattern of mental functioning.

ALVEOLI—The tiny air sacs of the lungs—The lungs contain millions of these alveoli. They fill up like balloons whenever the chest cavity is enlarged by the motion of the ribs and the diaphragm, and then collapse partially when the breath is exhaled. The alveoli are surrounded by minute blood vessels. Exchanges of oxygen and carbon dioxide take place through the very thin walls of the alveoli and blood vessels.

ANGINA PECTORIS—A painful symptom of a heart disorder—A pain in the chest which is experienced ordinarily when there is an unusual demand for blood in the heart muscle (myocardium), but the coronary arteries cannot supply it in adequate quantity.

ANTIBODIES—Natural substances that protect the body against a specific disease or infection—Antibodies are part of the body's natural immunity system. They destroy harmful bacteria and counteract the poisons produced by disease germs.

AROUSAL—The state of being alert, excited, and wakeful in contrast to quiescence and a state of sleep—The neural mechanisms that arouse the person to activity are set off by a stimulating event that usually comes from the external environment; however, internal activity, both physiological and neurological may also arouse the person to activity.

ATHEROSCLEROSIS—A condition associated with hardening of the arteries—When fatty and mineral deposits accumulate in the walls and on the inner surfaces of the arteries, the walls gradually become thickened and less elastic. The deposits may narrow the passageways so that the flow of blood is seriously curtailed.

AUTONOMIC NERVOUS SYSTEM—The part of the nervous system that regulates the involuntary activities of the tissues and organs of the body such as breathing, the beating of the heart, the rate of glandular activity, and the contraction and dilation of the blood vessels—It is actually made up of two systems: the sympathetic nervous system and the parasymphathetic nervous system. These systems check and balance each other so that the body can adjust to all types of situations and function effectively in time of stress.

BETA—The range of brain waves varying from 13 to 30 cycles per second.

BIOFEEDBACK—The process by which one can become aware of some of body's internal events of which one is not normally aware, through the use of some technical device, in order to learn to control some aspect of that event.

BLOOD PRESSURE—Pressure exerted by the circulating blood against the walls of the blood vessels—The pressure is greatest during the systole, when the heart contracts and forces blood into the arteries of the body. This maximum pressure is known as systolic pressure. During the diastole, when the heart muscle relaxes, the pressure drops to a minimum, which is called diastolic pressure. Blood pressure varies from person to person, as well as from time to time in the same person. It is influenced by general health, heredity, age, activity, and emotional state.

CARDIOVASCULAR SYSTEM—The system through which blood circulates—heart, arteries, capillaries and veins.

CATHARSIS—An outpouring of verbal expression that brings about release from tension.

CENTRAL NERVOUS SYSTEM—The brain and the spinal cord.

CHOLESTEROL—A chemical substance present in the blood, the brain and all other tissues throughout the body, as well as in much of the food we eat—Chemically it is a sterol, a complex secondary alcohol. It consists of white crystals, something like sugar, but it dissolves in fat and not in water. It is manufactured by the body, chiefly in the liver and adrenal glands.

COGNITIVE DISTORTION—A distorted notion about an object or event obtained through the normal cognitive processes but that is deviant from the normally held views of other people.

CONSCIOUSNESS—The totality of awareness of one's own thought processes and of external events—It is not an entity, an all-or-none condition, but rather a process and a continuum of experience.

CORTEX—An outer or covering layer of an organism or one of its parts.

COSMIC MEDITATION—Meditative experience in which the meditator integrates himself or herself with the cosmic nature of the universe—It is an altered state of consciousness in which the microcosmic man loses his ego identity and becomes one with the macrocosmic universe.

COSMOS—The orderly systematic universe.

DELTA—The range of brain waves varying from zero to 4 cycles per second.

DESENSITIZATION—The mental process of establishing a hierarchy of scenes of an increasingly anxiety-provoking quality related to a phobic or traumatic experience, while being in a physiologically relaxed state.

DUODENAL ULCER—An inflamed open sore on the mucous membrane lining of the duodenum, the part of the digestive tract adjoining the lower end of the stomach.

ELECTROCARDIOGRAM (ECG; EKG)—A tracing, or graph, made by minute electric impulses generated in the heart—The pattern produced by the impulses indicates whether the heart is in good condition or whether it is damaged, and to what degree. The instrument used to record the tracing is called an electrocardiograph.

ELECTROENCEPHALOGRAM (EEG)—A tracing, or graph, made by minute electric impulses generated in the brain, known as brain waves—The recorded brain waves are interpreted by a specialist to indicate various conditions of the brain. Brain waves are also indicative of the various states of existence, such as, waking, resting, dreaming and sleeping. The instrument used to record the tracing is called an eletroencephalograph.

EMOTIONAL TURBIDITY—The state of mind of a person who flares up spontaneously with an emotional outburst even at a seemingly trivial incident.

ENDOCRINE GLAND—Any of various glands, as the thyroid, adrenal, and pituitary glands, that secrete certain substances or hormones directly into the blood or lymph—ductless gland.

EPINEPHRINE—Another name for adrenaline, a hormone secreted by the adrenal glands.

EQUANIMITY—Evenness of mind or calm temper—The mental state transcending the emotional feelings of anger, fear, grief, and joy.

FIGHT-OR-FLIGHT RESPONSE—Psychophysical reaction to an inner or outer stress or a stressful event which literally prepares the individual for fighting or running away by increasing blood pressure, heart rate, breathing rate, body metabolism or rate of burning fuel and the flow of blood to the muscles of the arms and legs.

GENERAL ADAPTATION SYNDROME (GAS)—The process by which a feeling of psychological discomfort gains momentum—It is manifested in three stages. Stage 1 is an alarm reaction during which the sympathetic branch of the autonomic nervous system takes over with a resulting rise in heart rate and blood pressure. State 2 is a state of physiological resistance with the body's immune system brought into play. Stage 3 is the state of exhaustion when the defense system can no longer cope with the stress and loses its adaptation. The phrase, GAS, was introduced by Dr. Hans Selye.

GESTALT—An entire situation viewed from the emotional as well as the cognitive mode—A system of psychology which insists on seeing the individual as a whole, psychologically and physiologically.

GLYCOGEN—A polysaccharide (a complex starch) formed from glucose and found in various tissues but stored especially in the liver and muscles—Glucose is a monosaccharide which is the simplest structural unit of carbohydrate, one sugar unit.

HATHA YOGA—That part of the Yoga system that deals with physical postures and exercises.

HEMOGLOBIN—The oxygen-carrying substance of red blood cells, to which their color is due.

HERTZ—A unit of the rate of occurrence of an electromagnetic wave equal to one cycle per second.

HOMEOSTASIS—A tendency to stability in the normal body states— The four major organ systems responsible for maintaining the homeostasis of the body are the respiratory system, the digestive system, the urinary system, and the circulatory system.

HYPERTENSION—High blood pressure—When a person has a systolic pressure above 160 millimeters, he is usually considered to have high blood pressure or hypertension.

HYPNAGOGIC—Transition from waking to sleeping, accompanied by vivid imagery.

HYPOTHALAMUS—The portion of the middle part of the brain that is known to regulate body temperature and help control the functions of the internal organs.

IMMUNITY SYSTEM—The several lines of body defence which prevent and fight the entry of invading organisms, and which serve to maintain overall physical health.

MACROCOSM—The great world or universe; the universe considered as a whole.

MEDITATION—The act or process of meditating—serious contemplation or reflection; a state of deep physiological relaxation, accompanied by alpha and theta brain waves; a mental state of heightened awareness.

MICROCOSM—A little world—an individual man or a community that is a miniature universe or a world in itself.

MIGRAINE—A condition marked by recurrent severe headache often with nausea and vomiting.

NERVOUS BREAKDOWN—A vague, non-medical term for emotional illness, or a critical point in one, that comes on suddenly.

NERVOUS TENSION—Nervous strain, brought about by physical or psychological causes.

NEUROMUSCULAR HYPERTENSION—Undue muscular tension resulting from excessive stimulation and overworking of the muscle fibers.

NEUROPHYSIOLOGY—Branch of physiology which deals with the functional aspect of the nervous system, in particular, the investigation of the nature and transmission of the nerve impulse.

NICOTINE—A poisonous alkaloid that is the chief active principle of tobacco—Nicotine is an addictive drug that is absorbed from the lungs and acts mainly on the nervous system.

OMEGA EFFECT—The unique characteristic of the human mind that includes emotions, cognitive processes, subtle experiences, personal identity and consciousness, which can not be explained by behavioral sciences; that mental effect that distinguishes man from machine. The phrase, Omega Effect, was introduced by the British Scientist, Gordon Rattray Taylor.

OXYGEN DEBT—Inability of the body to supply the full amount of oxygen needed to produce the necessary energy to perform a physical task or a sustained exercise—The work done under this condition is called anaerobic work. During this period there is a build up of lactic acid in the blood stream which induces fatigue.

PARASYMPATHETIC NERVOUS SYSTEM—One part of the autonomic nervous system that acts as a balance to the other part, namely the sympathetic nervous system—Stimulation of various parasympathetic nerves causes the pupils of the eye to contract, causes the heart to beat more slowly, and produces other nonvoluntary reactions.

PEPTIC ULCER—An inflamed open sore on the mucous membrane lining of the stomach.

PHYSIOLOGICAL—Pertaining to that branch of biological science called physiology; concerned with the functioning of the structure and organs in a living organism.

PITUITARY GLAND—A very important endocrine gland in the body, also called hypophysis—The pituitary gland is a tiny mass of tissue attached by a thin stalk to the hypothalamus at the base of the brain.

PSYCHOANALYSIS—A method of studying and treating emotional and mental disorders, originally developed by the Austrian psychiatrist, Sigmund Freud, at the turn of the 20th century. It is one of a number of forms of psychotherapy. Psychoanalysis aims at bringing repressed memories, conflicts, and unconscious impulses into consciousness.

PSYCHOPHYSIOLOGICAL—Pertaining to both psychological and physiological factors—what affects the mind affects the body and vice versa.

RELAXATION RESPONSE (RR)—The natural and innate protective mechanism which is the anti-thesis of the fight-or-flight response—The relaxation response brings on bodily changes that decrease heart rate, lower metabolism, decrease the rate of breathing, and bring the body back into a healthier balance. The phrase, relaxation response, was introduced by Dr. Herbert Benson of the Harvard Medical School.

SATURATED FAT—Dietary fat made up of saturated fatty acids—When a fatty acid molecule is saturated with the maximum possible number of hydrogen atoms it can take, it is called a saturated fatty acid.

SELF-EXCELLENCE—The state of excellence of the totality of a person—body, mind, intellect, and the ability for humanistic interaction with others, which allows him or her to develop as a unique person to his or her fullest potential and lead a meaningful life of self-fulfillment (internally) and self-expression (externally)—Self-excellence is not an end, but a means and a way of life. The phrase, self-excellence, was introduced by the author.

SELF-HYPNOSIS—A sleep-like state, or trance, that is induced by one's own suggestion—It is an an altered state of consciousness.

SELF-IMAGE—The subjective image that one thinks oneself to be not only in personality but also in status, character or reputation, and physical appearance—Self-image plays a key role in the behavioral responses of individuals. It is not a static or fixed image; it is amenable to change and improvement.

SELF-PSYCHOANALYSIS—Psychoanalysis carried out by the subject himself or herself—see **PSYCHOANALYSIS**.

STRESS—A condition or state that manifests itself in changes which occur in the organs of the body or in the mental state of the individual—Stress is the consequence of conflict. Stress affects both physical and mental adaptation. See also **GENERAL ADAPTATION SYNDROME (GAS)**.

STRESSOR—An element or an event that comprises an unresolved conflict and produces stress.

SWABHAVA—The Sanskrit word for the subtle characteristic of uniqueness that is innate and inherent in every human mind—In those activities that are in tune with this characteristic, the person will be able to excel and feel good about himself or herself. It is the built-in direction for self-development. It is not the same as aptitude—the latter is liable to change, but Swabhava is not. See **UNIQUENESS CHARACTERISTIC**.

SYMPATHETIC NERVOUS SYSTEM—The counterpart of the parasympathetic nervous system—Together they constitute the autonomic nervous system. It regulates tissues not under voluntary control, e.g., glands, heart, and smooth muscle. See Parasympathetic Nervous System.

GLOSSARY

SYSTEMATIC DESENSITIZATION—See **DESENSITIZATION**.

TAR—A dark, odorous viscous liquid obtained by destructive distillation of organic materials, like coal and wood—It is contained in tobacco smoke and condenses into a sticky substance in the lungs.

TENSION—A word commonly used to refer to nervous strain—Tension may be induced due to physical or psychological reasons.

THETA—The range of brain waves varying from 4 to 7 cycles per second.

TRANSCENDENTAL MEDITATION (TM)—A form of meditation in which the person uses a subvocal utterance of a personal mantra, or sound, repeatedly and rhythmically, as a means of focusing attention inwardly—TM was introduced to the West by Maharishi Mahesh Yogi from India during the early sixties.

TRIGLYCERIDE—Biochemically, triglycerides are fats having 3 fatty acid molecules attached to each glycerol molecule—They are the most commonly consumed dietary fats, accounting for 95 percent of fat in food.

UNIQUENESS CHARACTERISTIC—See **SWABHAVA**.

UNSATURATED FAT—Dietary fat made up of unsaturated fatty acids—Unsaturated fatty acids are those that have less than the possible maximum number of hydrogen atoms attached to the carbon chain of the fatty acid molecule.

VISUALIZATION—A meditation process in which the person forms and holds a vivid mental image of an object, scene or a concept, and uses this imagery as the focus of passive concentration while being in a state of physiological relaxation.

YOGA—A Hindu theistic philosophy that aims at the integration of the individual soul with the Cosmic Soul or Spirit through self-realization and transcendence of all mundane activity of body, mind and will—The Yoga philosophy was systematized by the saint and philosopher of India, Pathanjali, in his *Yoga Sutra*.

INDEX

A
Accept and adapt, 126, 174
Adaptation, 5-6, 42-43, 121
Adrenal glands, 26-27, 31, 33, 36, 125, 181
Adrenaline, 27, 33, 36-37, 126, 181
Aerobic, 102-103, 181
Alcohol, 163-165
Alcoholic, 165, 175
Alpha waves, 31, 33, 114, 116, 121, 130, 181
Altered state of consciousness, 114
Alternate toe-touch, 97-98
American Medical Association, 161, 163, 166, 177
Amphetamines, 168
Anaerobic work, 102
Anger, 4, 11, 19, 24, 27, 33, 37, 43, 48, 61, 64, 87-88, 125-126, 142, 184
Angina pectoris, 51, 54, 182
Anxiety neurosis, 45
Arousal, 33, 182
Arteriosclerosis, 35, 49
Artery spasm, 36-37

A (Cont.)
Assertiveness, 148
Asthma, 48
Atherosclerosis, 35, 49, 54, 154
Attitude, 77, 79-80, 121, 135, 151, 174
Attitude modification, 121, 144, 151, 174
Autohypnosis, 114
Autonomic nervous system, 27, 29-30, 154, 182
Autosuggestion, 114, 119

B
Backache, 62, 64
Barbiturates, 168
Behavior, 27, 40-41, 48, 70, 120, 124-125, 142-144, 146, 149, 151, 174
Behavioral modification, 58, 121, 144, 151, 174
Benson, Herbert, 49, 128, 130, 177
Beta waves, 31, 33, 114, 116, 182
Bhagavad Gita, 179
Bhirud, Ravindranath, 110
Biofeedback, 126
Blood, 25, 27, 29, 34-36, 92, 155, 157, 164-165, 171

B (Cont.)

Blood cholesterol level, 35, 154-155, 157
Blood lactate, 92
Blood pressure, 20, 27, 29, 34, 49, 114, 160-161, 169, 171, 182
Blood-sugar levels, 21, 34-35
Body-fat, 155, 157, 159
Body-mind unity, 7, 8, 15, 47
Body weight, 161-162
Brain, 27, 29, 31-33
Brain waves, 31, 33, 114, 116, 130
Breathing, 10, 34, 105, 108-109, 117, 125, 129, 171
Buddhism, 9

C

Cade, Maxwell, 130, 177
Caloric intake, 161, 163
Calories, 163
Cancer, 171
Campbell, Gregg, 103, 177
Cannon, Walter, 33
Capillaries, 37, 51
Carbohydrates, 154
Cardiovascular system, 49, 51-52, 91, 110
Carnegie, Dale, 141, 147-148, 177
Catharsis, 143-145, 183
Cells, 51, 155, 161, 164-165
Central nervous system, 27-28, 31, 164
Cerebral cortex, 165
Cholesterol, 35, 154-157
Circulation, blood, 51, 54, 155
Cognitive dissonance, 80

C (Cont.)

Cognitive distortion, 79-80, 183
Cognitive process, 142
Colitis, 59
Commitment, 81, 84-85
Concentration, 105, 129
Conflict, 21-22, 41, 48, 119-120
Confucius, 19
Cooper, Kenneth, 102, 177
Consciousness, 10, 105, 183
Contemplation, 113, 118, 120
Coronary arteries, 51, 53
Cosmic consciousness, 10, 14
Coxhead, Nona, 130, 177
Creativity, 10-11, 131

D

Death, 67, 126
Delta waves, 33, 115-116, 183
Depression, 59-60
Desensitization, 126-127, 184
Diastolic blood pressure, 49
Diet, 153, 157, 160, 163
Digestive system, 48, 56
Discipline, 73, 75, 173
Dreams, 115
Drugs, 164, 167-169

E

ECP Balance, 91-92
Elbow push, 94
Electrocardiogram (ECG), 110, 184
Electroencephalograph (EEG), 114, 184
Emotion management, 124
Emotional turbidity, 73, 78-79, 184
Emotions, 4, 11, 19, 24, 27, 33-34 37, 43, 59, 61, 65, 87, 124, 126, 142-143, 148, 174

INDEX

E (Cont.)
Emphysema, 171
Endocrine glands, 25, 27, 48, 184
Enthusiasm, 81, 85-86
Epinephrine, *see* Adrenaline
Equanimity, 3, 7-8, 11, 14, 19, 173, 184
Equilibrium, 10
Excellence, 8, 15, 91, 110, 131, 141, 153, 175
Exercises, 91-92, 94-95, 102-103, 108-110, 174
Eysenck, H. J., 68
F
Fatigue, 60, 62-63, 91, 105, 171
Fats, 34-35, 154-155, 157, 159-160, 175
Fear, 4, 11, 19, 24, 27, 33, 37, 43, 61, 64, 87, 124-125, 142, 184
Feedback, 136-137
Fight-or-flight response, 33, 35-36, 49, 184
Fink, D. H., 46
Fitness, 96-97, 102, 105
Flutter-kick, 100-101
Foods, 153-157, 159
Fredenburgh, Franz, 61, 177
Freud, Sigmund, 40-41, 45, 48, 144
Friedman, M., 68, 177
Frustration, 4, 44, 58
G
Galton, 20, 178
General adaptation syndrome (GAS), 20, 34, 43, 185
Gestalt therapy, 185
Glands, 25, 27, 33, 43, 188
Goal setting, 131-134
Goals, 131-134, 173-174

G (Cont.)
Grief, 4, 11, 24, 37, 61, 65, 87, 126, 142, 184,
Guilt, 48
Guthrie, Helen, 160, 178
H
Haft, Jacob, 37
Handpush, 95
Happiness, 11-12, 15, 43, 65
Hardening of the arteries, *see* Atherosclerosis
Hate, 43, 119
Hatha Yoga, 91, 105, 109, 185
Headaches, 4, 21, 48, 57-58, 165
Heart, 29, 36-37, 49-51, 53-54, 110
Heart attack, 50, 54
Heart disease, 51, 54
Hemorrhage, brain, 54-55
Heroin, 168
High blood pressure, 20, 34-35, 48-49, 160, 181, 185
Hitchcock, Kathleen, 91, 105
Hockey, Robert, 94
Homeostasis, 7, 10, 31, 34, 173, 178, 185
Hormones, 25, 27, 33-35
Hughes, Charles, 131, 178
Human sensitivity, 143
Hunger, 154
Hypertension, *see* High blood pressure
Hypnagogic state, 115
Hypnosis, 114
Hypothalamus, 25, 27, 29, 31-33, 36, 154, 185
I
"I" concept, 7, 10-11
Identity, 11, 14

I (Cont.)
Imagery, 121, 138
Immune system, 43, 186
Insomnia, 21
Intellect, 10-12, 15
Interpersonal relationship, 141-143, 145-148
Intuition, 10-11
Involuntary nervous system, *see* Autonomic nervous system
Isometric contraction, 94
Isometric exercises, 94
Isotonic contraction, 94-95

J
Jealousy, 43
Job stress, 67
Jogging, 102
Joy, 43, 61, 65
Jump rope, 102-104

K
Kidney, 30, 56

L
Lactic acid, 92
Levels of consciousness, 114
Life, 5, 10, 12-13, 19, 75, 173, 176
Limbic system, 43
Lincoln, Abraham, 137
Liver, 30, 165
Love, 43, 65, 151
Low blood pressure, 122, 167
LSD, 168
Lungs, 169-172

M
Macrocosm, 9-10, 120, 186
Macintyre, Christine, 92
Mahesh Yogi, Maharishi, 189
Maltz, Maxwell, 113, 119, 121, 135, 178

M (Cont.)
Mantras, 189
Maslow, Abraham, 124
McKain, Robert, 81, 83, 119, 145, 178
Meditation, 113-115, 117, 122, 124, 126, 186, 189
Memory, 31, 165
Metabolism, 34, 128, 165
Michelangelo, 173
Microcosm, 9-10, 120, 186
Migraine, 58, 186
Miller, B. F., 20, 178
Mind, 7-8, 10-12, 25, 39-41, 47-48, 77-79, 113, 115, 117, 119-120, 122, 124, 127, 129-131, 138, 145, 153, 173, 178
Mind/body interaction, 7, 25, 47, 104
Mitchell, Curtis, 104, 178
Money, 59, 79-80
Mood, 59
Morgan, Clifford, 25, 178
Morphine, 168
Motivation, 75-76, 81, 85, 135-136
Muscle tension, 62-63
Myocardial infarction, 54

N
Narcotics, 168
Needleman, Jacob, 9, 178
Nervous system, 27-31, 121, 164, 168, 182-183, 187
Nervous tension, 46, 186
Neurosis, 45, 69, 79-80
Noradrenaline, 27, 34
Norepinephrine, 27
Nutrients, 51, 153-154, 163

O

Omega Effect, 40-41, 186
Opium, 168
Organism, 33
Ornish, Dean, 36
Overlearning, 139
Oxygen, 51, 54, 56, 102-103, 169, 171
Oxygen debt, 102, 186

P

Parasympathetic nervous system, 29, 154, 187
Passive attitude, 129
Passive concentration, 122
Pathanjali, Saint, 189
Patience, 73, 78
Pelletier, Kenneth, 122, 178
Perception, 124
Personality, 40, 67-70
Physical fitness, 94, 96-97, 102, 105
Pituitary gland, 25-26
Platelet clumping, 36-37
Pleasure, 11-13
Pollution, 167
Polyunsaturated, fats, 159-160
Positive mental attitude, 76-77
Posture, 62, 105
Procrastination, 76
Protein, 154, 163
P/S ratio, 159-160
Psyche, 39
Psychoanalysis, 41, 144, 187
Psychology, 25, 39, 178
Psychophysical, 175, 187
Psychosomatic illnesses, 48
Psychotherapy, 41
Purpose in life, 73-74

R

Relaxation, 33, 37, 92, 102, 109, 128, 167
Relaxation response, 128-130, 177, 187
Religion, 9, 113
Repression, 45
Rest, 76
Reticular core, 31
Rogers, Carl, 143
Role playing, 138-139
Rope, jump, 97, 102-104
Rosenman, R. H., 68, 177
Running, 97, 102

S

Sanzotta, Donald, 144, 178
Saturated fats, 159, 163, 175, 187
Self-acceptance, 113, 118-120
Self-actualization, 124
Self-confidence, 81-83, 148
Self-esteem, 40, 88, 143, 146-148
Self-excellence, 3, 8-9, 14-15, 73, 81-84, 86, 88, 119, 173, 175-176, 188
Self-expression, 5, 76, 175
Self-fulfillment, 6, 76, 175
Self-image, 7-8, 45, 64, 69, 77-79, 82, 84, 86, 88, 113, 118, 122, 135, 139, 142, 148, 161, 174, 188
Self-psychoanalysis, 113, 120-121
Selye, Hans, 3, 5-6, 19-20, 34, 178, 185
Serum-cholesterol level, 35, 157
Seven laws of human behavior, 142, 151
Seven laws of stress, 20-21

S (Cont.)
Seven laws of success, 136-137
Sex, 79-80
Skill-learning, 138
Skipping, *see* Rope, jump
Sleep, 115
Smoking, 167, 169-172
States of consciousness, 114
Stomach, 29, 56-67
Stress, 3-9, 14, 19-25, 27, 31, 33-39, 41-43, 45, 47-49, 54, 56-62, 64-68, 78, 178
Stress-related disorders, 6, 47
Stressors, 4, 20, 188
Stroke, 54-56
Subliminal, 69
Success, 80
Swabhava, 188
Sympathetic nervous system, 29, 154, 188
Systematic desensitization, 126-127
Systolic blood pressure, 49

T
Taylor, G. R., 40, 178, 186
Thiruvalluvar, Saint, 153, 179
Triglyceride, 155, 157-158, 189
Tuke, Daniel, 47

U
Ulcers, 6, 47-48, 55-57, 184, 187
Unconscious mind, 40
Uniqueness characteristic, 12, 189
Unsaturated fat, 157-160, 163, 189
Upanishads, 9, 167

V
V-Sit, 95-96
Vascular system, 51
Veins, 51
Visualization, 118, 121-122, 138, 189
Voluntary nervous system, 27-29

W
Walking, 62
Wave length, 31, 33, 114-115
Webster, 19, 148
Weight, body, 161-162
Weight control, 161
Wessel, Janet, 92
Wolpe, Joseph, 126
Women, 22

Y
Yoga, 105-109, 178, 189

Z
Zimbardo, Philip, 39, 115, 178

About the Author

Dr. Shanmugam A. Swami, born on May 30, 1928 in India, received his formal education in 3 continents. He holds a bachelor's degree in civil engineering from the University of Madras, India, a master's degree from the University of New South Wales, Sydney, Australia, and a doctorate degree from Purdue University, Lafayette, Indiana, USA. An avid traveler, he has travelled around the globe, widely in India, Europe, Canada, and the USA, visiting as many as 49 states.

He holds the view that a planned, goal-oriented living is necessary to bring forth the best efforts of the individual for both self-fulfillment (internally) and self-expression (externally), no matter in what station of life one is. He emphasizes the need for the subjective inquiry of the self for discovering one's own potential for success in life and the need for conscientious effort on the part of the individual to unearth this innate potential.

Dr. Swami has presented many seminars on stress management and goal-oriented living to the public and professional organizations.

An in-depth reader of the philosophies of the east and west, he believes that the ultimate human destiny lies on the *self-excellence* of the human race—the state of excellence of the graceful development of the finite microcosmic man merging himself with the infinite macrocosmic milieu without being a threat to the fellow human being.

Dr. Swami serves as a professor of civil engineering in the West Virginia Institute of Technology since 1968. He is married and has one son.

Colophon

Self-Excellence:
*Key to Preventive Stress Management
and Goal Oriented Living*

This book was designed by the author and produced by Minibook Publishing Co., Montgomery, WV.

The text type—11 on 13 Times Roman—was set on AM Varityper phototypesetter.

The text paper is Wausau cream white 60-pound opaque offset.

The printing was done by Richard L. Hopkins at the Pioneer Press of West Virginia, Inc., Terra Alta, WV.

The binding was done by John H. Dekker & Sons of Grand Rapids, Michigan.